Pacific
RAILROAD

BRIAN SOLOMON

MBI Publishing Company

Acknowledgments

Growing up in the eastern United States, I viewed the SP from a far for many years. My first experience with SP was a ride along the Coast Line from Oakland to Los Angeles. Later I moved to California and explored SP in much greater depth. I am indebted to Brian Jennison and J. D. Schmid for detailed tours of SP and for their contagious enthusiasm. Brian is also fellow SP scholar and helped me with aspects of this text and provided photographs. T. S. Hoover accompanied me on numerous SP and Rio Grande excursions, lending his technical expertise on many occasions. Brian Rutherford introduced me to the Santa Cruz branch and helped in detailed planning for a trip to the Oregon Cascades. Mel Patrick, a fellow traveler and photographer, provided his unique insight and valuable research material. Robert A. Buck, and George C. Corey lent their knowledge on steam locomotives. Gerald Hook and F. L. Becht introduced me to SP operations in Louisiana. My father Richard Jay Solomon, who joined me on several visits to the SP, was especially helpful by lending me the use of his library and assisting in proofreading. And thanks to Mike Schafer, Steve Esposito, and Maureene Gulbrandsen of Andover Junction Publications, the producer of this book, for their crucial roles in the production of the book.

Many talented photographers have contributed to this book and their fine work is much appreciated. Joe McMillan and Fred Matthews were especially generous with their vintage material. Lastly, I would like to thank the employees of Southern Pacific for their friendly, professional, and courteous treatment over the years. Bob Hoppe, Jack Martin, and Bart Nadeau in particular made working with the Southern Pacific Railroad a uniquely enjoyable experience.

—*Brian Solomon*
Monson, Massachusetts

First published in 1999 by MBI Publishing Company, 729 Prospect Avenue, PO Box 1, Osceola, WI 54020 USA

© Andover Junction Publications, 1999

Book design and layout by Mike Schafer and Maureene D. Gulbrandsen/Andover Junction Publications, Andover, New Jersey, and Lee, Illinois.

Edited by Mike Schafer/Andover Junction Publications

MBI Publishing Company books are also available at discounts in bulk quantity for industrial or sales-promotional use. For details write to Special Sales Manager at Motorbooks International Wholesalers & Distributors, 729 Prospect Avenue, PO Box 1, Osceola, Wi 54020-0001 USA..

Library of Congress Cataloging-in-Publication Data Available
ISBN 0-7603-0614-1

FRONT COVER: *Southern Pacific colors adorn a former Rio Grande Electro-Motive diesel leading a potash train on the Cane Creek branch in eastern Utah in 1997. The Denver & Rio Grande Western was one of SP's expansion endeavors of the late twentieth century.* Brian Solomon

FRONTISPIECE: *Dating from the 1870s, Southern Pacific's famous setting-sun logo adorned rolling stock, published items, and signage to the end of the railroad in 1996. Housed at the California State Railroad Museum in Sacramento, restored SP Electro-Motive E9 6051 sports the venerable emblem on its nose.* Brian Solomon

TITLE PAGE: *A pair of Electro-Motive GP9s clad in Southern Pacific's celebrated "Black Widow" paint scheme splits the semaphores at Tacna, Arizona, in 1960 with a reefer train.* Gordon Glattenberg

CONTENTS PAGE: *Southern Pacific's Cab-Forward articulated steam locomotives (often referred to as "cab-aheads" by SP crews) were unique to the railroad and became an icon of SP's steam era. Here at Mojave, California, in 1949, Class AC-11 Cab-Forward No. 4255 leaves the passing siding with the second section of train 804. The smoke from the train's helper can be seen toward the rear.* J. R. Quinn collection

BACK COVER: *Southern Pacific GS-4-class Daylight steam locomotive No. 4449 holds court with SP 0-6-0 switcher 1269 and Electro-Motive E9 No. 6051 at the California State Railroad Museum in Sacramento in May 1984.* Mike Schafer

Printed in Hong Kong

Contents

Introduction

Southern Pacific's Natron Cutoff climbs through Pengra Pass in the Oregon Cascades on a ciruitous alignment constructed in the 1920s. On a misty June 14, 1994, a westbound freight (moving geographically east) passes the west switch at Fields as it enters tunnel 15 on its climb to Cascade Summit. *Brian Solomon*

Southern Pacific, that an all-encompassing name. It's a name that covers the intricate corporate fabric of a complex industrial enterprise during the course of one and a quarter centuries. Known for its distinguished visionaries, flamboyant leaders, dedicated employees, distinctive trains, and unusual locomotives, Southern Pacific is perhaps best defined by the geography it conquered and served. Mountains, deserts, canyons, valleys, rivers, lakes and oceans. No American railroad—or perhaps any railroad—encountered such a diversity of geographical obstacles. From its beginnings, the railroad proposed to surmount natural barriers so great as to bring ridicule upon its founders, yet its tracks prevailed. Blizzards, avalanches, floods, landslides, earthquakes, war—no railroad persevered over greater adversity and disruption than the fabled Southern Pacific.

Southern Pacific's unique operating environments encompassed a variety of superlative situations for which it is remembered including: thirty miles of Sierra snowsheds designed to protect track from snow as deep as 20 feet; perilously steep, tortuous grades; more than a hundred miles of oceanside running; a trestle (and later a fill) across the Great Salt Lake; the lowest main line in North America running many miles well below sea level; more tunnels than any other railroad in North America—more than nearly all other Western railroads combined.

Southern Pacific crossed mountains everywhere it went, and its Donner Pass, Tehachapi, Cuesta grades are legendary. Even its lesser-known grades, Viewland Hill, Ridge Hill, Moor Hill, and Montgomery Pass inspire visions of grand vistas and the struggle of man and machine over nature. Helpers, synonymous with Southern Pacific operations, were found all over the system in every form imaginable. It was an awesome daily drama. Cinders blasting skyward from their stacks, a quartet of cab-ahead Mallets—spaced mid-train in a heavy fruit block—ascend the Sierra. Baldwin road-switchers shoving hard on a heavy lumber-laden drag crawl upgrade in Oregon's Siskiyou Mountains. Seventeen EMD GP9s in three groups—head-end, mid-train, and tail-end—roar upgrade as they lift a 13,500-ton ore train toward Apex on Beaumont Hill in

Southern California. Their dynamic brakes howling and bathed in the purple haze of brakeshoe smoke, three SD45s diesels descend Cuesta, restraining dozens fully loaded wooden beet racks fore and aft.

Southern Pacific's prosperity was integral with California's rapid growth, and the early history of the railroad and state are inseparable. For many years, SP headquarters was located at 65 Market Street in San Francisco—known in later years as 1 Market Plaza—just a few blocks away from the San Francisco Ferry building. Southern Pacific's timetable was strictly bi-directional, and the ferry building was that point farthest west on the railroad. Trains rolling toward San Francisco, regardless of destination or actual direction were deemed westbound while those moving away from San Francisco were eastbound. SP's directional dichotomy has led to considerable confusion among casual observers and others unfamiliar with the intimacies of its operations.

Although SP and its affiliated lines connected Portland, Oregon, and New Orleans, Louisiana; St. Louis, Missouri, and Dallas/Ft. Worth, Texas; and reached more than 1,000 miles into Mexico, Southern Pacific operations were largely centered on California. SP and its subsidiaries operated to every corner of the state, from the remote, windswept, sage-covered Modoc plateau, to the rocky crags of Carriso Gorge. "Espee" tracks wound up the Sacramento, Truckee, and Eel River canyons, rolled along Caliente Creek, and San Pablo Bay, and served the Salinas, Sacramento, San Joaquin and Imperial valleys. Electric interurban trains rolled to Venice Beach, across the Oakland Bay Bridge, and through the verdant hills of Marin County north of San Francisco.

East of El Paso to New Orleans, SP operations were handled by its Texas & New Orleans subsidiary, a company blended with its parent in later years. In the 1930s SP reached eastward through Arkansas to Memphis and St. Louis by way of the St. Louis Southwestern, a line known universally by its nickname, Cotton Belt. In its last decade as an independent carrier, SP and Rio Grande were joined, giving access to Denver, Kansas City, and finally Chicago. Purists will forever distinguish the "true" SP from its later days of integration with Rio Grande. Yet, SP trains rolled in the shadow of the Book Cliffs, through Glenwood Canyon, over Tennessee Pass, and across the Front Range of the Rockies through the famed Moffat Tunnel. As strange as it may seem, SP freight rolled across Illinois cornfields past General Railway Signal color position-light signals—hardware installed for Baltimore & Ohio-controlled Alton Railroad.

Southern Pacific lines are now under operation and control of its long time Overland interchange partner and one-time owner under Harriman, Union Pacific. Although many time-honored SP trademarks have faded from the scene—cab-ahead articulateds, streamlined *Daylight* passenger trains, Pacific Fruit Express reefers, lower-quadrant semaphores, wooden snowsheds, and the signature sweep of oscillating headlights—the railroad remains. Trains still roll past the golden grass and twisted oaks of Tehachapi, through tunnels and snowsheds in the Sierra and Cascades, across the Arizona desert and over Paisano Pass, but while the defining geography of the former Southern Pacific remains, and the railroad lives under a new name, it is not, and never will be the same. Long live the memory of the late, great Southern Pacific!

On the eve of the Southern Pacific's demise as an entity railroad, train PBASM (Pine Bluff–Alton & Southern Merchandise) awaits a green light at Valley Junction, Sauget, Illinois, on January 11, 1995. *Scott Muskopf*

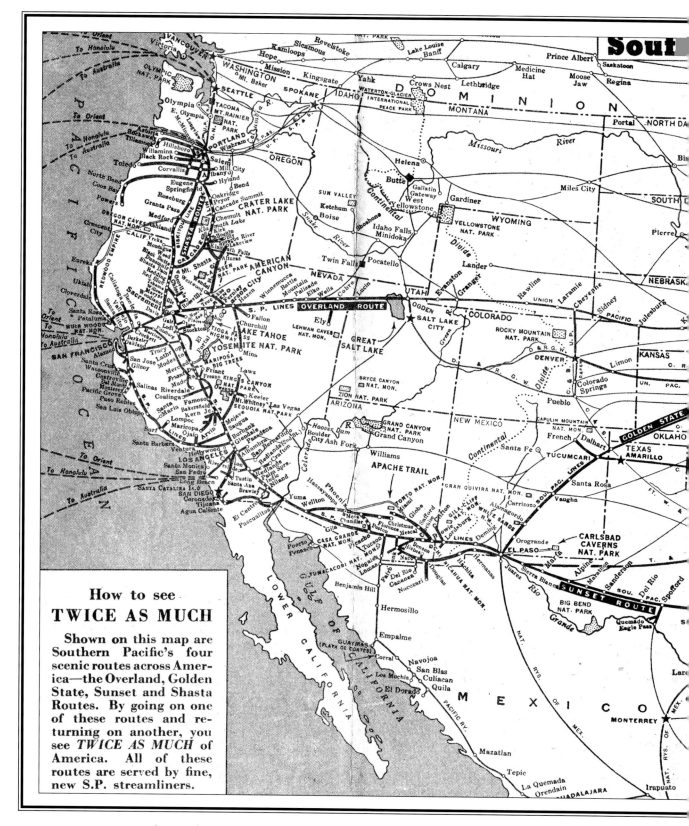

How to see
TWICE AS MUCH

Shown on this map are Southern Pacific's four scenic routes across America—the Overland, Golden State, Sunset and Shasta Routes. By going on one of these routes and returning on another, you see *TWICE AS MUCH* of America. All of these routes are served by fine, new S.P. streamliners.

This map from an SP public passenger timetable dates from the first half of the twentieth century and shows the railroad prior to its hefty expansion later in the century. Note how each of the railroad's four most-famous routes—Overland, Sunset, Golden State, and Shasta—have been labeled. *Andover Junction archives*

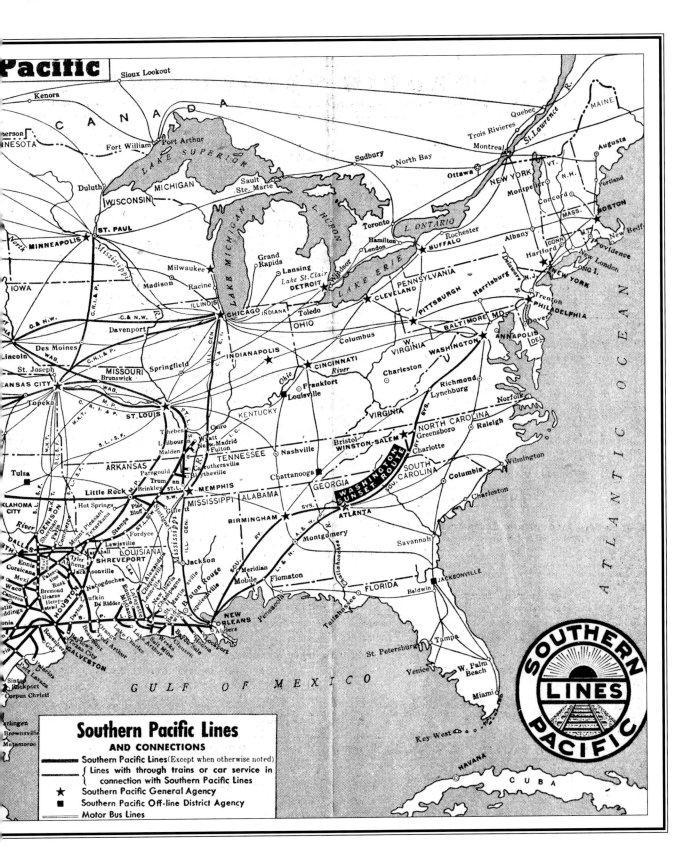

Southern Pacific Lines

Southern Pacific Lines
AND CONNECTIONS

——— Southern Pacific Lines (Except when otherwise noted)
{ Lines with through trains or car service in
connection with Southern Pacific Lines
★ Southern Pacific General Agency
■ Southern Pacific Off-line District Agency
===== Motor Bus Lines

The face of the railroad that for decades dominated Western transportation: Southern Pacific. *Joe McMillan*

Chapter 1

Southern Pacific: Building an Empire

1862–1900

Southern Pacific's intricate, complex story has not one beginning but many. Numerous companies, each that ultimately came under Southern Pacific control, has its own tale to tell; this account is just a brief summary of what became the modern Southern Pacific—that which was folded into the Union Pacific in 1996—and of the people involved.

POTS OF GOLD IN THE GOLDEN STATE

Fortune seekers flocked to California by the thousands following the discovery of gold in the Sierra foothills in 1849. Although many hoped to find their fortune in gold, others hoped to profit through business. As the population of California grew, businesses blossomed and flourished. The railroad was still in its infancy, yet by this time it had clearly demonstrated that it was the most effective land transportation system available. In 1852 the Secretary of War had a congressional mandate to locate the best route for a railroad to the Pacific shores. That same year California's first railroad, the Sacramento Valley, was chartered. In 1854 the line made the fortuitous decision to hire Theodore Judah as its chief engineer. Judah, among the most talented railway engineers in the U.S., had completed several difficult projects in the East and was seeking a more ambitious challenge. The SV operated its first train on August 17, 1855, over a short segment of track, and six months later it completed a 23-mile line into the foothills, running from Sacramento to Folsom.

Judah was not satisfied with the limited scope of this pioneering California railroad and soon adopted the building of a transcontinental line as his life quest. The multi-talented Judah was instrumental in making this monumental project a reality. No railroad had ever crossed such formidable barriers as the California Sierra and the deserts east of the mountains, and skepticism for the project often outweighed real physical barriers. Yet through years of hard work, surveying in the Sierra, playing politics in Sacramento, San Francisco, and Washington D.C., and stirring up public and financial interest, Judah got the first transcontinental railroad under way.

Judah's crucial role in this effort cannot be overplayed. He personally laid out most of railroad over Donner Pass, drew up an early original Central Pacific charter, gathered investors—including the four pivotal businessmen that would bring the project to completion—personally lobbied Congress and the President of the United States, and helped draft the Pacific Railroad Act that authorized the building of the transcontinental railroad.

In 1861, Judah convinced four successful Sacramento business owners, Collis P. Huntington, Leland Stanford, Charles Crocker, and Mark Hopkins—later popularly known as the Big Four—to support the railroad. That same year, Leland Stanford was elected as governor of California. In July 1862, President Lincoln signed the Pacific Railroad Act—legislation that provided both federal land grants and cash to Union Pacific and Central Pacific for building the railroad. Central Pacific construction began in Sacramento in a lively public ceremony presided over by Leland Stanford on January 8, 1863; the first rails were laid 10 months later. The Big Four had

One of the most notable events in railroad history occurred in one of the most remote regions of the country which the event would unite. At lonely Promontory, Utah, the Central Pacific and Union Pacific joined iron on May 10, 1869, opening the first official transcontinental rail line in America. The 1904 opening of the Lucin Cutoff eventually doomed the original route. *Mike Schafer*

Central Pacific was built from west to east, beginning at Sacramento. The main waiting room of SP's Sacramento depot—now served by Amtrak—features a large mural depicting a public ceremony presided upon by Leland Stanford marking the beginning of Central Pacific construction in 1863. *Brian Solomon*

sufficient money and political connections to build Judah's railroad, but they embraced business methods that Judah questioned, and shortly after the railroad was under way they began to force him out of the project. Dissatisfied with their handling of railroad affairs and furious at being excluded from the railroad he worked so hard to build, Judah had hopes of buying out the Big Four out and completing the railroad in accordance with his vision. Unfortunately for Judah, he died in November 1863, before he could act. He was only 37.

The Big Four collective would run the railroad enterprise for the next few decades. Their business affairs were complex and often deliberately convoluted. For this reason it is simpler to refer to their railroad enterprises as the Big Four rather than delineate each specific subsidiary, holding company, or controlling property. Each of the four played a crucial role in the growth and development of first Central Pacific and later Southern Pacific and its controlled companies. Huntington served as the business intellect, Stanford as company politician, Crocker as builder, and Hopkins as accountant.

In its first few years Central Pacific suffered from insufficient funding and made slow eastward progress building into the Sierra. By 1865 the railroad had only reached Auburn, just 35 miles east of Sacramento. That year, the railroad made the unprecedented move of hiring an estimated 14,000 Chinese laborers for construction in the Sierra to ease an extreme labor shortage. Construction in the Sierra proved more difficult than anticipated, and progress was further slowed by several exceptionally harsh winters and snowfall much deeper than predicted by the optimistic Judah. Tracks reached Donner Summit in July 1867. Central Pacific and Union Pacific were racing the railroad to completion, as each line received considerable land and subsidy for

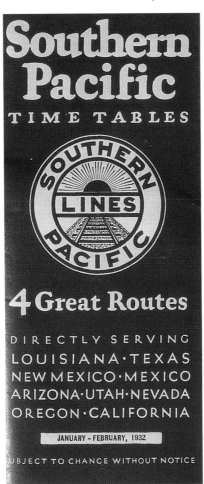

each mile finished. While CP inched along in the Sierra, UP plodded across the plains. Time was running short, and to push the railroad ahead to make faster eastward progress against the rapidly advancing Union Pacific, Central Pacific forces jumped ahead of Sierra construction teams in 1867 and began building eastward across the Nevada desert. The line over Donner was finally completed in May 1868. A year later on May 10, 1869, CP and UP formally met in the very famous, publicly-staged, golden spike ceremony at Promontory, Utah. Champaign flowed freely as Leland Stanford and other dignitaries greeted the public and made speeches—and history. A telegraph operator relayed the railroads' completion to the world and this event has become the most remembered—and most pictured—in railroad history. Regular freight and passenger service commenced over the new line a few days later.

Although completion of the transcontinental line was the Big Four's most widely known accomplishment, it was really just the first step in building a comprehensive transportation system. In just a few years they were building tracks in all directions; what they didn't build, they bought. They played a shrewd game of law, politics, and finances that allowed their railroad enterprise to grow and prosper faster than any other in the West. Although they frequently violated the comparatively loose ethical business standards of the time, their dealings and antics appear outright criminal by contemporary standards. They bought legislation, paid off politicians, subverted their enemies, and either bought out or crushed anyone who stood in their way. They manipulated construction contracts, often hiring and paying themselves to build their own lines. They took advantage of liberal federal land grants and took title to millions of acres of land. Over the course of just a few years they

came to completely dominate transportation in California and played a large role in many other states as well.

Huntington was brash and unapologetic about his company's dealings. He did whatever was necessary for the railroad to survive and thrive. As an excellent judge of human character, Huntington rarely found himself on the wrong side of a bad deal. He was the also longest lived of the Big Four, surviving until 1900; Hopkins died in 1878, Crocker in 1888, and Stanford in 1893. Dealings between the Big Four were not always amiable. Late in life Huntington and Stanford had a vicious public falling out from which they never recovered. Yet these four men were very tight in their dealings, and few others had insight as to their plans or finances. Their domination of California business is legendary and their gross abuses of power—both real and perceived— left a legacy of distrust, suspicion, and hatred that lingered for decades after they had passed from the scene.

SOUTHERN PACIFIC

While the Big Four were pushing their Central Pacific over Donner Pass, another railroad scheme was in the works. In June 1864 a railroad called the San Francisco & San Jose opened on the San Francisco Peninsula. Just 18 months later, principals behind the SF&SJ incorporated the Southern Pacific, a line initially envisioned to link San Francisco and San Diego by way of Los Angeles and ultimately connect someday with a line to be built west from the Missouri River.

After its original charter, the railroad's scheme was reconfigured to serve as the Western partner in a transcontinental scheme, similar to that abuilding between Sacramento and Omaha. Congress authorized Southern Pacific to build east from San Francisco to the Colorado River where it was to meet the Atlantic & Pacific. Initially SP investigated building its main line southeasterly of San Jose, passing through Gilroy and over Pacheco Pass into the San Joaquin Valley, then over the Tehachapi Mountains and across the Mojave desert. SP acquired the SF&SJ and planned to put its scheme into motion. By March 1869 SP had reached Gilroy, a little more than 30 miles south of San Jose. Yet, Southern Pacific's independence was very short lived. The savvy Big Four were wary of transportation competition and by 1868 looked to buy SP for themselves.

continued on page 18

High point—literally—of the joint Chicago & North Western–Union Pacific–Southern Pacific Overland Route between Chicago and the Pacific Ocean was SP's segment over Donner Pass in California's Sierra Range. Though sunny and peaceful looking on this spring day in 1981 as a westbound freight negotiates the Pass near Donner Lake (background), the Sierra crossing is fraught with treacherous winter weather that has trapped both pioneer travelers and modern streamliners. *Jim Boyd*

DONNER PASS

At one time more than 30 miles of wooden snowshed protected Donner from unusually heavy snow, but by the mid 1950s most of the sheds had been removed, leaving short segments at crucial locations. On May 27, 1970, a westbound pokes out of Tunnel No. 6—the old summit tunnel—at Norden, California. *Joe McMillan*

Donner Pass was undoubtedly one of the most famous locations on the Southern Pacific—a place of legend known for its extreme adversity and dramatic railroading. Where other SP mountain crossings can claim steeper grades, heavier traffic, and more sinuous track arrangements than Donner, no other grade is as old or as formidable as this storied mountain crossing. Donner's exceptionally long eastbound grade—96 miles—rising from near sea level in California's Central Valley to a summit 7,000 feet high in the Sierra would test the mettle of any railroader, but what places Donner in a class by itself is its exceptionally harsh and often unpredictable winter weather. The pass is named for the ill-fated Donner party snowbound there trying to reach California decades before the railroad was built.

In the late 1850s and early 1860s Theodore D. Judah, the far-sighted visionary of the Central Pacific, surveyed much of the line over Donner with aid of his faithful wife Anna. Judah's early efforts were frustrated when he couldn't locate an obvious route that would bring the tracks from the American River Canyon all the way to Donner Summit. He was aided by his friend Dr. Strong of Dutch Flat who found a natural "bridge" at Smart Ridge that could carry the line from the American River basin to the that of the Yuba River and thence to Donner Summit. Although Judah died in

1863, his railroad was built. It crossed Donner Pass in 1868 and ultimately connected with the Union Pacific in 1869—a line known as the Overland Route after the famous Overland Trail that followed a similar path.

Although a brilliant engineer, Judah had seriously misjudged the annual snowfall on Donner Pass, and his successors faced operational headaches beyond Judah's worse nightmares. Dozens of miles of snowshed were constructed to keep the railroad fluid during times of heavy snow, and ultimately there were more than 30 miles of shed between Emigrant Gap and Andover (on the east slope of Donner west of Truckee). In addition, a fleet of plows were kept at the ready to cope with blizzards and snow slides. Ultimately the development of the Leslie rotary snowplow made keeping Donner open to traffic in even the worst weather a plausible task. Although once the standard snow-fighting weapon, today rotary snowplows are used only to clear the very heaviest snow and do not run on a regular basis because they are so costly to operate. In modern times SP maintained a fleet of Jordan spreaders and flangers for winter service on Donner in addition to its rotary plows.

Under E. H. Harriman, Donner Pass matured in to a modern mountain railroad. He implemented numerous improvements that changed the character of the line and made it more fluid and easier to operate. Harriman was notorious for railway safety (today, Harriman Safety awards are presented to railroads with superlative safety record) and instituted block signals on much of the Overland Route. However to cope with the unique complexities of mountain operations over the pass with its extensive snowsheds and tunnels, an electric staff traffic-control system was established. Staff systems were used extensively overseas but did not enjoy widespread application in the U.S., but Donner's staff system, which controlled 98 route-miles, was the most extensive such application on a American railroad. Gradually the staff system was replaced as the line was converted to double-track operation.

Adding a second track over Donner—another Harriman improvement—was more complicated than simply grading another few feet of right-of-way adjacent to the existing track. In many places, especially on the west slope between Rocklin and Colfax and on the east slope between Lawton and Floriston, a new alignment was constructed to ease the gradient and curvature. Donner double-tracking included a new, shorter crossing of the line's namesake pass, featuring a new summit tunnel, nearly two miles long—the longest on the traditional SP. Antitrust issues and SP's legal battles delayed the Donner Pass double tracking, and as a result it was not finished until the mid 1920s.

During World War II as many as 100 moves a day passed through the summit sheds at Norden. Freight and passenger trains poured westward to aid the war effort in the Pacific. After the war, traffic subsided somewhat yet remained robust, but during the next 40 years SP gradually shifted traffic away from the Overland Route. Other changes affected traffic moving over Donner. The Bay Area slowly lost much of the heavy industry it had gained during the war, and it lost its premier port status. Donner had been the primary route for perishable traffic. Fruits and vegetable grown in California and Oregon's verdant valleys for con-

sumption in the rest of the country were loaded into refrigerated boxcars and dispatched over Donner at regular intervals. The development of highway transportation eroded SP's share of fruit traffic out of California, but as late as the mid 1970s Roseville Yard was still sending an average three solid "fruit blocks" a day over Donner during peak harvest. Today, while the days of regular produce trains have passed, it is still possible to see large cuts of refrigerator cars moving east across the Sierra.

In 1981, SP's longtime Overland Route partner, Union Pacific, bought the Western Pacific and shifted the bulk of its remaining Overland traffic to WP's Salt Lake City—Bay Area line, leaving SP's once-busy mountain crossing now nearly devoid of traffic. During the 1980s only a handful of daily trains would cross via Norden, but by the end of the decade there was a moderate increase in Donner traffic following the joining Southern Pacific and Rio Grande in 1988, and by 1990 the railroad was operating about five or six freights each way every 24 hours. Yet the line's secondary status was obvious.

In 1993, years of traffic deficiency caught up with the famous Sierra crossing. Ed Moyers, looking to improve SP's ailing railroad fortunes, decided the underutilized Overland Route would benefit from the same pruning treatment that he successfully applied to the Illinois Central. Two short segments of double track were removed over Donner: the original 1868 crossing of the summit between Norden and Shed 47, and between Switch 9 (east of Emigrant Gap) and Shed 10 west of Cisco. A great deal more double track was converted to single track in the desert east of Reno. Unfortunately Moyers, like Judah, had grossly underestimated the power of a Sierra winter. These issued combined with capacity problems have prompted Donner's new owner Union Pacific to considered rebuilding some double track over Donner.

Winter on Donner Pass means snow, and lots of it. When the drifts get too high for the flangers and spreaders to handle, the call goes out for the ultimate snow-fighting equipment, the rotary snowplows. Here a double-ended plow set works its way uphill at Yuba Pass following a late storm on April 1, 1982. *Brian Jennison*

Continued from page 15

The dealings of the Big Four were rarely straightforward, and it's uncertain exactly what transpired, but by 1870 Southern Pacific and associated properties were consolidated into the Southern Pacific Railroad Company, a company under the control of Central Pacific interests. From 1870 onward, Central Pacific and Southern Pacific were financially, personally, and operationally intertwined. Where one ended and the other began mattered only on the ledgers of accountants and lawyers. For all practical purposes, the two were one and the same. Years later SP would convincingly argue this point in court.

A few months after the completion of Central Pacific's transcontinental line between Sacramento and Utah, the Big Four reached the Bay Area by way of the Western Pacific (no connection with George Gould's railroad of the same name built decades later), a line built via Tracy and over the Coast Range via Altamont Pass. Western Pacific's operations were melded with those of Central Pacific in 1870. The Big Four decided against pursuing SP's planned Pacheco Pass crossing and instead directed their construction forces to build southward through the San Joaquin Valley from a junction on the WP at Lathrop. At that time this valley was largely open, uninhabited territory, and as the railroad pushed its way south, towns sprung up along the line, and many of the present-day communities in the San Joaquin Valley owe their existence to the railroads. Rail service to

continued on page 21

The original Southern Pacific pushed south from San Francisco to Los Angeles via the San Joaquin Valley and entered the Los Angeles Basin by way of the Tehachapi Mountains. During the post-World War II years, Cab-Forward steam locomotive 4103, a Class AC-4 built by Baldwin in 1928, moves a merchandise train off the San Joaquin Valley route into the Tehachapi Mountains. *Donald Duke*

Six Harriman-era heavyweight suburban coaches make up "commute" train (as they are known in the Bay Area) No. 150 ambling away from its Menlo Park station stop along the old San Francisco & San Jose line in 1956. The original Southern Pacific bought the SF&SJ in the late 1860s as part of its scheme to build a transcontinental route via the southern tier of the U.S. *Donald Duke*

TEHACHAPI AND THE LOOP

Tehachapi has been described as the greatest train-watching place in the world, and few would argue. The intrigue of Tehachapi is its unique combination of scenery, cosmic weather, rugged grades, looping track, and the variety of intense heavy freight action. To the railroads, however, Tehachapi is an enormous operational headache—a terrible bottleneck wrought with grade-related difficulties. For 67 miles two busy railroads share the same set of tracks over the mountains, making for one of most heavily traveled, single-track mountain crossings in America.

Although these mountains posed a rugged, formidable crossing, this pass was judged the best route by SP engineers. SP was building the second transcontinental line in a southeasterly direction and reached the Tehachapis in 1876. William Hood designed the route and, following the contours of the land, planned a series of horseshoe curves and loops to gain elevation. Nine miles from the summit at a location now known as Walong, he made the unprecedented decision to loop the tracks right over themselves, gaining 77 feet and maintaining a steady upbound gradient. Tracks reached Tehachapi Summit—elevation 4,025 feet above sea level—in July 1876, and the railroad was completed through from San Francisco to Los Angeles on September 5, 1876. A last-spike ceremony was held at Lang, California, in Soledad Canyon.

For nearly a quarter century, SP had the Tehachapis to itself. However, competitor Santa Fe was contemplating building its own line through the Tehachapis to the Bay Area and surveyed its own sinuous crossing. In 1899, before Santa Fe made serious construction plans, SP acquiesced to allow Santa Fe trackage rights over its Tehachapi crossing. Santa Fe (now Burlington Northern & Santa Fe) rails join SP's at Mojave and leave again on the west side of the mountain at Kern Junction in Bakersfield.

The compensated eastbound ruling grade is 2.52 percent, just slightly steeper than SP's Donner Pass crossing; westbound the compensated grade is comparatively mild at 1.36 percent. What makes the climb difficult in addition to the long sustained steep grade are the numerous tight

An SP work train heads into the siding at Walong on the lower end of Tehachapi Loop as a Santa Fe train clears the upper end of the loop in July 1969. *Mike Schafer*

curves, frequent tunnels, and significant sections of single track that often force heavy trains to stop while climbing the hill to allow traffic to pass. No train moves up or down Tehachapi quickly. For many years freight trains were limited to just 18 mph and passenger trains just 25 mph. Helpers are the rule and very few trains cross the mountain unassisted. In steam days it was not unusual to see a heavy freight climbing the hill with five or six locomotives spread throughout the train. Running light helpers back to the base of the grade adds to the operational difficulties in the Tehachapis. Prior to the advent of CTC—first installed during World War II—helpers would tend to collect at the top of the mountain. When traffic eased, helpers would be gathered together (the record was 24 locomotives) and all run back down the mountain at once. Today Tehachapi is one of the last places where manned mid-train helpers are still a daily event and one of the last places where trains use three sets of manned locomotives to make it over the grade.

The line has been a busy route for many years. Even before Santa Fe trains began using the route, SP discovered its value as both a through route to Los Angeles and as a transcontinental line. By the early 1920s the line was extremely congested, forcing SP to build some sections of double track to improve the traffic flow. In 1925, the two railroads moved some 19 million tons of freight over the mountain, equaling approximately 1,400 freight cars a day. The route saw its peak passenger traffic in the 1920s but has been known largely as a freight route in modern times. Since the advent of Amtrak in 1971, there have been no regularly scheduled passenger trains over Tehachapi (Amtrak buses can do the Bakersfield–L.A. run faster) and the railroads have resisted efforts to introduce new passenger services to this congested mountain crossing.

Although the SP built, owned, operated, and maintained Tehachapi, toward the end of SP's independent operation, tenant carrier Santa Fe had stolen the show by running between two and three times more trains over Tehachapi each day than SP.

Continued from page 18

Modesto (20 miles southeast of Lathrop) began in November 1870 and tracks had reached another 90 miles to Fresno by May 1872, and finally in November 1874 it reached the established community of Bakersfield (named for Colonel Thomas Baker).

To survey the route over the Tehachapis, the Big Four employed the services of railroad engineer William Hood. He proved well-skilled and ultimately laid out much of SP's line all the way to San Antonio, Texas, as well as other well known-lines. Hood had a long productive career with SP. He was promoted to chief engineer following the death of Samuel Montague in 1883 and served with the company in that capacity until the 1920s.

Los Angeles—in the 1870s a relatively small city of less than 10,000—enticed Southern Pacific to place it on the new transcontinental route despite the obvious detour such a line would require, and the railroad was completed between San Francisco and L.A. on September 5, 1876. A year later SP reached the Colorado River at Yuma, Arizona. The Big Four

finagled arrangements to build beyond SP's original charter and continued east across Arizona and New Mexico on the auspices that it would meet Jay Gould's Texas & Pacific building its way west from Marshall, Texas. SP reached Tucson in March 1880, Lordsburg, New Mexico, in October, and El Paso on May 19, 1881. By this time the Big Four had one of the most experienced railroad construction crews in the world who had been building railroads across some of the most difficult terrain in America for 18 years. East of El Paso, construction continued, though under the flag of the Galveston, Harrisburg & San Antonio, a company in which the Big Four had bought control in order to reach Texas and New Orleans while circumventing Gould's T&P. The plan worked, and although a connection with the T&P had indeed been effected at Sierra Blanca, Texas, in January 1882, SP's through route to New Orleans was completed in January 1883, and thus the Sunset Route was in place. Lines both in and east of

continued on page 24

SP's San Joaquin Valley Line took the railroad through the heart of one of California's most fertile regions—a bountiful source of perishable traffic for Southern Pacific as well as Santa Fe. In 1947, one of SP's big 4-6-0s built in 1913 storms past the Stockton depot with general freight. *Fred Matthews*

Southern Pacific will forever be closely associated with California and Oregon, but those two states did not have a monopoly on scenery. Illustrating that Texas can be big on scenery as well as other things, we take you to Paisano Pass, Texas. This area exhibits some of the most stunning desert scenery on the old Texas & New Orleans. On May 11, 1992, westbound symbol freight HOWCM (Houston– West Colton Manifest) negotiates the pass. *George S. Pitarys*

Six Electro-Motive GP35s lead the Douglas (Arizona) branch local on the Sunset Route main line at Pantano, Arizona, east of Tuscon in 1985. SP had a comprehensive network of lines in southern Arizona, including alternative mainline routes and numerous branches. Some Sunset Route passenger trains operated via Benson, Arizona, while others operated via Douglas near the Mexican border. *George S. Pitarys*

Continued from page 21

Texas were under separate management to comply with Texas laws requiring local control of lines within the state. After 1927, SP's conglomeration of Texas and Louisiana lines were operated under the umbrella of its Texas & New Orleans subsidiary.

The Sunset route was SP's longest traditional line—essentially running from coast to coast—connecting the L.A. basin on the Pacific Ocean with New Orleans at the Gulf of Mexico. Aptly named, the Sunset Route traverses some of the most arid terrain in the continental U.S., and one is likely to see the setting sun over these tracks nearly any day of the year. The line climbs east out of the L.A. Basin by way of Beaumont Hill and then drops into the Imperial Valley where it has the significance of being the longest (and one of the only) sections of American main line running below sea level. From Yuma the Sunset Route continues across the desert to New Mexico where east of Lords-

burg it enjoys the lowest railroad crossing of the Continental Divide in the lower 48 states—4,584 feet—more than a mile lower than Denver & Rio Grande Western's Tennessee Pass crossing. El Paso is the junction with the Golden State Route, location of a significant freight yard, and in traditional times the eastern limits of SP's Pacific Lines. East of El Paso the railroad was operated by the Texas & New Orleans subsidiary. Paisano Pass is just a few miles beyond El Paso at 5,074 feet above sea level—the highest point on the SP between Portland, Oregon, and New Orleans.

Although the Sunset Route held a secondary role during its early years, it ultimately supplanted the Overland Route as Southern Pacific's premier transcontinental main line. This shift in emphasis is reflected by the adoption of train Nos. 1 and 2 for the *Sunset Limited* in the 1930s, numbers long held by premier Overland Route trains. In its later years, the

Sunset was SP's bread-and-butter line. Some of SP's traditional lines, including the once-busy Overland Route, languished from lack of traffic, but the Sunset bristled with trains and suffered from insufficient capacity. It was so choked with freight—largely container traffic heading toward the booming ports at Los Angeles and Long Beach—that by the mid 1990s SP management made the decision to double-track portions of the line that had never seen more than a single set of rails.

Looking Toward Oregon

The Big Four's California & Oregon built toward Marysville, California, in 1869 and reached Redding by 1872. Here the rails ended for more than a decade, in part because the Panic of 1873 brought a temporary halt to many railway schemes across the country and because the Big Four did not feel an urgency in reaching Oregon. In the mid-1880s interest in a direct Oregon main line resumed, and the Big Four pushed the C&O line north to meet with the Oregon & California that was building south from Portland. Although the O&C reached Eugene in 1871 and Roseburg, Oregon, in 1872, it ceased construction for nearly a decade and did not reach Ashland, Oregon, until 1884. Finally the Big Four took control of the O&C and the Oregon main line was completed in 1887.

In a tinted postcard postmarked March 27, 1909, SP's *California Limited* pauses at Shasta Springs, California, in the upper Sacramento River Valley. SP's original main line from California to Oregon was completed in 1887. *Brian Jennison collection*

THE CARSON & COLORADO

There was still much talc traffic on the remaining portion of the old Carson & Colorado in 1952 when this eastbound narrow-gauge freight wheeled through Mt. Whitney, California—and a desert sandstorm. *Fred Matthews*

One of the most interesting and more colorful Southern Pacific operations was its three-foot gauge Carson & Colorado line that ran on the east side of the Sierra. Although never a significant source of traffic, SP's desert narrow gauge was one of the only American common carrier narrow-gauge lines that survived long enough to operate diesels, and one of the last Class I narrow-gauge railways.

Constructed in the 1880s as an extension of the Virginia & Truckee, the Carson & Colorado ran from Mound House, Nevada (near Carson City), 293 miles south to Keeler, California, by way of a spectacular mountain crossing at Montgomery Pass and the Owens Valley. The C&C was built at the height of the American narrow-gauge movement when many new railroads adopted three-foot gauge instead of standard gauge as a way of reducing construction and operating costs. The line foundered as an independent railroad and was purchased in 1900 by the SP which envisioned using the line as part of a new route to connect Salt Lake City and Los Angeles. Although SP intended to convert the whole route to standard gauge, it never fol-lowed through, and much of the C&C remained as a narrow-gauge operation, although SP officially dropped the C&C name a few years after it assumed control. SP built standard-gauge branches to connect with both ends of the narrow gauge. Later it converted the line north of Mina, Nevada, to standard gauge.

Traffic on the line was never robust and by the 1930s SP was looking to trim the route. It closed the line between Mina, Nevada, and Benton, California, over Montgomery Pass in 1938 and left the line derelict. It finally lifted the rails during World War II, at which time it abandoned an additional 31 miles, leaving just 70 miles of operational narrow gauge between Laws (near Bishop, California) and Keeler. This remaining segment survived for another two decades, long enough for SP to introduce single, custom-built General Electric diesel-electric locomotives. For nearly five years steam and diesel coexisted on the narrow gauge, and narrow-gauge steam outlived Southern Pacific's main-line operations. The last of the old C&C narrow gauge was finally abandoned in 1960.

Under a backdrop of sparkling conifers, a Portland-bound freight howls through the Sacramento River canyon above Redding, California, in 1984.
Mike Schafer

On St. Patrick's Day 1884, the Big Four consolidated various properties, including Central Pacific and some steamship companies, under the umbrella of the Southern Pacific Company, which was incorporated in Kentucky for strategic legal reasons. At this time the Big Four owned and controlled more than 5,000 railroad route-miles and had successfully fended off all serious competition in their vast territory.

As far transportation was concerned, SP was the only show in town. But then the Big Four began to feel competitive pressure: In 1884 Union Pacific reached Portland, and a year earlier the Santa Fe had landed across from Needles, California. Southern Pacific built a line across the desert from Mojave to Needles in an effort to thwart further Santa Fe encroachment. But Santa Fe had the upper hand and initiated a peculiar business deal whereby SP ended up trading its Mojave-Needles line to Santa Fe for railway lines that SP wanted in Mexico. Santa Fe wasted no time in seeking California markets and by 1885 had completed a through route between San Diego, Los Angeles, and Chicago—a move that soon precipitated a vicious rate war between the two roads.

FINER! FASTER! Two *Daylights* a day, each way, now serve Los Angeles, San Francisco and intermediate points on new and faster schedules. These million dollar trains, four of them, provide a morning and noon departure from each terminal.

The Morning *Daylight* leaves San Francisco and Los Angeles at 8:15 a.m. and reaches destination at 5:45 p.m. The Noon *Daylight* leaves at 12 noon, and reaches destination at 9:40 p.m.

Southern Pacific's first twin *Daylights* (inaugurated March 21, 1937) quickly became so popular that they frequently were unable to accommodate all the travelers who clamored to ride them. So two magnificent new *Daylights* took their place on January 10, 1940. Then the original trains were restored to shining newness and now they are again in service on the new Noon schedule.

We wish we could take you through these *Daylights* and show you why so many people consider them the most beautiful trains in the world. We'd like to show you their big, soft reclining chairs cushioned with foam rubber and their enormous windows that give you the sensation of being out of doors. We'd like to have you enjoy one of their famous meals in the sumptuous Dining Car, or in the Coffee Shop. Prices are as low as 45c for luncheon or dinner in the Coffee Shop. And we'd like to take you into the sensational *Daylight* Tavern Car, curtained with Venetian blinds and lined with cozy leather booths.

Then we'd like to show you the lovely Coast Line that these trains travel by daylight between Los Angeles and San Francisco—the "Route of the Missions"—through the rich Santa Clara and Salinas Valleys, over rugged mountain ranges and along the very edge of the Pacific Ocean for 113 miles of breath-taking beauty.

But since we can't show you all these sights and scenes in person, we'll do the next best thing and show them to you in the natural color photographs inside this folder. Fares and detailed schedules are given on the back.

Southern Pacific

In the early 1930s SP President Angus McDonald envisioned a fleet of gorgeous trains rolling over his railroad as a way of rejuvenating passenger revenues. By the mid 1940s the SP was operating a fleet of streamlined Daylight trains advertised as "the most beautiful trains in the world." *Joe Welsh collection*

Chapter 2

Southern Pacific in the Twentieth Century

1900-1996

By the mid-1890s, C. P. Huntington, then the last surviving member of the famous "Big Four" quadrumvirate (Chapter 1), was among the richest men in America. In 1890 his fortune was worth an estimated $40 million. The SP controlled more than 8,000 route-miles in the U.S. and Mexico and was considered the most extensive transportation company in the world. At the turn of the century, SP was close to completing one of its long-planned routes—its famous Coast Line connecting San Francisco and Los Angeles by way of San Luis Obispo. The final gap was finally closed in 1901.

THE HARRIMAN ERA

As the century drew to a close, a then-relative newcomer entered the Western railroad scene who would forever change the railroad map. Edward H. Harriman took control of the bankrupt Union Pacific in 1897, a line that had suffered under the ownership of Jay Gould. In just a few years Harriman awed industry watchers and Wall Street investors by turning the company around. Soon he was looking to further expand and improve his transportation system and approached the aged Huntington about purchasing the Central Pacific. Huntington refused Harriman, but when Huntington died a short while later, Harriman wasted no time in seeking not just the Central Pacific, which was his primary objective, but the entire Southern Pacific system. Through skillful stock acquisition and business maneuvering, Harriman acquired more than 45 percent control of SP by 1901 at which time he uttered one of his most remember sayings "We have bought not only a railroad, but an empire."

Harriman's control of SP was relatively brief, but in a fairly short time he implemented a great many improvements that helped shape the character of the railroad in the twentieth century. Although SP was in good physical shape when Harriman acquired it, it suffered from antique construction and traffic congestion, particularly on the crucial Overland Route that Harriman hoped to exploit. He wasted no time in making an assessment of his new property, and, based on the suggestions of SP General Manager Julius Kruttschnitt, Harriman quickly authorized millions of dollars for badly needed improvements. Harriman is celebrated for implementing major engineering projects including: the Lucin Cutoff (see sidebar), the Bayshore Cutoff, Montalvo Cutoff (a significant line relocation on the Coast Line between Burbank and Montalvo by way of Santa Susana Pass), and the double tracking of the Overland Route. In addition to these highly visible projects, SP under Harriman made numerous other noteworthy improvements. It built and extended numerous sidings, rebuilt and improved dozens of bridges, laid significantly heavier rail on nearly half its routes, reballasted some 1,000 miles of track, installed 27 million new cross ties, purchased 540 new locomotives—many built to standardized designs—and ordered nearly 9,000 new freight cars. Another lasting Harriman-era improvement was one of the first wide-scale applications of automatic block signals. Harriman had a great concern for safety and equipped many SP main lines with protective Union Switch & Signal lower-quadrant semaphores—some of which survived to the end of the century—and for many years SP boasted

SP's famous Coast Line route was completed just after the turn of the century. As its name implied and this 1990 view dramatically confirms, the lower 150 miles of the route hugged the shore of the Pacific Ocean. In this scene, a sugar beet train rolls railroad west up the Coast Line at Gaviota, California. The "roots" (as beets were called by crews) were synonymous with Coast Line operations for many years. *Phil Gosney*

the most miles of signaled main line in America. When Harriman died prematurely on Sept. 9, 1909, SP was in dramatically better shape than when he bought it. Had he lived to see his railroad vision realized, one wonders what super-railroad he might have made of Southern Pacific.

LEGAL PROBLEMS

Following Southern Pacific's Harriman prosperity, the railroad became entangled in legal battles that dragged out over the next 15 years, and as the courts decided SP's fate, the railroad lay in limbo. Work was suspended on improvements initiated during the Harriman era until after the legal actions were settled. It was a significant period in the railroad's history and a turning point in its relationship with UP.

In 1908 the U.S. government sued to separate Union Pacific and Southern Pacific on the grounds that the combination was in violation of the Sherman Anti-Trust Act of 1890. The case spent nearly five years in the courts; in December 1912 the Supreme Court ruled to separate the two companies. Yet, this was only the beginning of SP's problems. Union Pacific protested the Southern Pacific-Central Pacific union and the government brought action against SP in an effort to separate those two companies. The advent of World War I and federal control of the American Railroads during the war delayed a court settlement, but in the 1920s the court battle resumed. This delay saved the SP-CP union because following the war, new legislation was passed providing the Interstate Commerce Commission—the regulatory agency that oversaw railroad issues—with significantly greater power. The battle over the SP-CP separation became a highly polarized issue that resulted in some unlikely allies. Traditional foes of Southern Pacific rallied for SP's cause while SP's one-time partner UP waged a nasty propaganda campaign encouraging SP's dismemberment. Union Pacific's selfish motives were transparent—it wanted Central Pacific for itself to compete directly with SP for California traffic. SP's Julius Kruttschnitt, who had risen through he ranks of the company and worked many years under the both the Big Four and Harriman, fought hard to save his railroad. Separating the Central Pacific would have destroyed everything he had worked for years to achieve. According to Don Hofsommer in his book *Southern Pacific 1900-1985*, Kruttschnitt argued that CP and SP were "interdependent, having been conceived, constructed, and operated as one connected whole." President Wilson, the U.S. attorney general, and the U.S. Supreme Court disagreed, and in May 1922 the Supreme Court ordered a separation of CP and SP. However, this was not the last battle.

In February 1923 the ICC with its new powers found Southern Pacific control of Central Pacific to be in the public interest. The governing body thus authorized Central Pacific to remain part of the Southern Pacific while imposing conditions that ensured SP and UP would remain partners on the Overland Route, and SP would not divert Overland traffic via other routes.

Following this crucial decision, SP resumed Harriman-inspired improvements and entered a new period of construction and prosperity. It completed Overland Route double-tracking and made an agreement with the Western Pacific to maintain the "paired track" arrangement set up during World War I that was felt to be mutually beneficial to both railroads. The agreement combined the two parallel, but often non-adjacent, single-track main lines for 183 miles across the Nevada desert between Weso (near Winnemucca) and Alazon (near Wells) to provide essentially a double-track

Among the numerous improvements ushered in with SP's Harriman era was the Bayshore Cutoff, a new shortcut into downtown San Francisco for SP's main line up the Peninsula. Built early in the twentieth century, the new route utilized a series of tunnels, fills, and cuts that straightened and shortened the route, making train operations —such as this outbound commute run in 1984— faster and more efficient. *Mike Schafer*

THE LUCIN CUTOFF

A trio of Electro-Motive SDs led by a unit clad in the short-lived Southern Pacific-Santa merger scheme skim across the Lucin Cutoff near Promontory Point, Utah, with a westbound freight in October 1986. *Brian Jennison*

High on a bluff at Lakeside, Utah—not a town, but a point along the railroad—looking east across the Great Salt Lake you can watch the distant headlight of a westbound freight appear to crawl up out of the water. This is one of the few places where you can clearly perceive the curvature of the earth. It might be 45 minutes from the time you spot a train making its way across the lake until it finally passes you at speed. The Great Salt Lake is among the most amazing places on the planet to watch trains. Everyone knows about the famous spike ceremony at Promontory where the Union Pacific and Central Pacific formally met on May 10, 1869. Promontory is often confused with Promontory *Point*, a promenade many miles to the south that reaches in to the lake. When standing at Lakeside, you can see Promontory Point 21 miles to the east and the tracks continuing across the lake beyond.

The original Central Pacific line was constructed in haste to reach as far east as possible to meet the Union Pacific. The railroads received hefty federal subsidies for each mile completed and were racing to claim the most number of miles, so building high-quality track along the most efficient routing was not a prime consideration. Where the two lines met was the not a practical spot for interchange yards, so, shortly after the completion of the line, the interchange point was moved east from Promontory to Ogden.

When Harriman acquired Southern Pacific in 1901, one of his primary objectives was to obtain the Central Pacific transcontinental line which he felt was a natural extension of his Union Pacific. When he acquired control of the properties, neither line was in superlative shape, and he embarked on a serious rebuilding of both railroads. Even before Harriman, C. P. Huntington had considered relocating the Central Pacific route across the Great Salt Lake. Initially, Harriman was unconvinced a line directly across the water was the best choice, but he ultimately approved the plan, and on March 8, 1904 the Lucin Cutoff opened—103 miles of new line including 15 miles of fill and an astounding 23 miles of trestle. It had taken 45 miles out of the Overland Route, eliminated many curves, and reduced the grade. Despite this, the original line through Promontory remained in service until 1942 when SP staged a removal ceremony comparable to the famous Golden Spike event to publicize its commitment to a war effort scrap-metal drive. Interestingly in the mid-1950s, SP management considered rebuilding the line around the lake when the 50-year-old trestle needed replacement. Instead the railroad chose to build a fill across the lake and dumped millions of tons of earth into the water. The fill opened in July 1959. Less than 25 years later SP was faced with raising the fill when, during one of the wettest seasons in recorded history, the level of the lake began to rise. Although abandonment of the Lucin Cutoff was strongly considered by railroad management, the railroad chose to retain the line. Today, SP's Salt Lake crossing is a vital part of Union Pacific's Central Corridor and often preferred over UP's parallel former-Western Pacific line which just skirts the lake to the south.

The Northwestern Pacific was one of several expansion-related acquisitions during the Harriman era. The scenic line, which ran north from the Bay Area some 280 miles to Eureka, California, remained a subsidiary of SP until the northern portion was sold to other interests in the 1980s. On a clear, bright May 24, 1970, NWP's then-only passenger train—a 145-mile run between Willits and Eureka—rolls past Island Mountain in the Eel River Canyon. SP used its only Budd Rail Diesel Car for the service. Service south of Willits to San Francisco was in later years provided by connecting buses. *Joe McMillan*

main line. Southern Pacific also completed several important Oregon projects conceived during the Harriman Era, notably the Natron Cutoff and the Modoc line.

Kruttschnitt, who had led the company since 1913, retired in 1925 after seeing the company through its long legal difficulties. The railroad was back on the road to prosperity: freight traffic was up and new routes were under construction. Unlike earlier leaders, Kruttschnitt recognized the value of public relations and worked tirelessly to improve SP's public image. Sadly, he never enjoyed his well-deserved retirement, dying unexpectedly only days after he left the railroad for which he had worked most of his life. The entire railroad mourned his loss and trains all over the vast SP paused as a sign of respect for Kruttschnitt.

Southern Pacific F7s cross a truss bridge near Hunter, Nevada on October 9, 1964. The SP and WP jointly operated their parallel (though not always adjacent) main lines as "paired track" between Weso (near Winnemucca) and Alazon, Nevada. Trains of both railroads generally would use WP tracks eastbound and SP tracks westbound. *Gordon Glattenberg*

In the 1920s Southern Pacific purchased the El Paso & Southwestern, a line that controlled the El Paso–Tucumcari segment of the Golden State Route (Rock Island actually owned from Tucumcari to Santa Rosa, New Mexico, but did not operate past Tucumcari). Following the dissolution of the Rock Island, SP through its Cotton Belt subsidiary picked the Rock's route east from Tucumcari to Kansas City and developed the Golden State Route as an intermodal corridor. On May 12, 1992, a Long Beach–East St. Louis intermodal train rolls past lower-quadrant semaphores east of Carrizozo, New Mexico. *George S. Pitarys*

Southern Pacific's Early Twentieth Century Expansion

Under Harriman, and in the years following its favorable ICC ruling, Southern Pacific added numerous new lines and subsidiaries to its empire in addition the newly built lines previously discussed. In 1903 SP acquired a 50 percent interest in Pacific Electric (see chapter 3) and bought full control seven years later. Pushing east from San Diego, SP joined forces with the Spreckles sugar interests in 1906 to build the San Diego & Eastern along the Mexican boarder, and the line was completed to El Centro, California, by way of the spectacular Carriso Gorge in 1919. As a subsidiary of the SP, the SD&E became the San Diego & Arizona Eastern. In 1907 SP and Santa Fe bought joint control of the Northwestern Pacific, consolidating a number of smaller railroads operating north of San Francisco. In the 1920s SP assumed complete ownership of the NWP.

Once SP was free from its legal separation hassles, it moved to secure the El Paso & Southwestern, a conglomeration of smaller railroads in Arizona, New Mexico, and Mexico controlled by the Phelps Dodge copper interests. This line made up a crucial portion of the Golden State route—a connection with the Chicago, Rock Island & Pacific at Tucumcari— but by the mid 1920s, appeared to be planning its own route to the coast. In 1924 SP acquired the EP&SW, thus simultaneously cementing its Golden State Route connections, expanding capacity on the Sunset Route between Tucson and El Paso, and eliminating potential competition for California traffic from the Rock Island. Early in the 1930s, SP improved its eastward connections by acquiring control of the St. Louis Southwestern, better known as the Cotton Belt, which gave SP a Texas connection to the St. Louis and Memphis gateways. Under SP, Cotton Belt retained considerable autonomy and was treated differently than most other affiliated companies.

DEPRESSION, WAR, AND PROSPERITY

The Great Depression had a disastrous impact on the American economy, many companies folded, millions of people were out of work, and numerous railroads became insolvent. Although SP suffered from a dramatic loss of traffic and was forced to significantly curtail its operations, lay off thousands of loyal employees, and dispose of more than 700 miles of unprofitable track, SP survived the Depression as a solvent company and compared to other lines was in reasonable financial shape.

If there was a gold lining for the SP during the 1930s, it was painted red, orange, and black. In 1937 SP climbed aboard the streamliner bandwagon, introducing what would quickly become one of the most beautiful streamliners to grace U.S. rails: the *Daylight* of 1937. The new trains did their job, enticing travelers to return to the rails, and soon SP established a whole network of *Daylight* trains and other streamliners.

World War II presented all American railroads with enormous amounts of freight and passenger traffic, and SP's strategic position on the West Coast made it a primary carrier of military supplies and personnel, giving it an especially heavy wartime burden. During the war SP was the third-largest freight hauler in the nation, exceeded only by the Pennsylvania Railroad and New York Central. Southern Pacific moved roughly five times more people in 1944 than it did in 1939 and hauled more military trains than any other American railroad. At the height of the conflict, more than 112,000 people worked for SP, an all-time high for the railroad.

Following the war, SP enjoyed robust peacetime traffic, largely as a result of the wartime buildup of California industry as well as California's continued population growth. However, although SP's freight business boomed, its passenger business slowly waned.

Under the leadership of D. J. Russell and others, SP rebuilt and modernized the railroad turning it into modern efficient transportation system. SP replaced its aging locomotive fleet by purchasing more than a 1,000 new diesel-electrics in less than a decade. It modernized yards and main lines and streamlined operations. In the 1940s and 1950s SP discontinued lightly used and unprofitable passenger trains such as those that traversed the San Diego & Arizona Eastern, and shed itself of its last electric suburban passenger operations. By the late

continued on page 41

Carriso Gorge on the San Diego & Arizona Eastern ranked among the most spectacular portions of the SP. On April 17, 1966, three Electro-Motive GP9s and a GP20 lead a freight across the tall wooden trestle near Tunnel 15 in Carriso Gorge. The track alignment elsewhere through the gorge is evident above the train where the right-of-way clings to the side of the chasm. *Gordon Glattenberg*

37

SP TO OREGON
THE SISKIYOU LINE AND THE NATRON CUTOFF

The Siskiyou, Southern Pacific's first main line to Oregon, is remarkable for its improbable profile, spectacular scenery, and long survival despite its eventual redundancy as a main line. The north end from Portland to Ashland, Oregon, was constructed by the Oregon & California, a company controlled by Henry Villard, known for his influence in Portland's business affairs and involvement in numerous railroad projects including the Northern Pacific. Big Four interests directed by C. P. Huntington constructed the south end of the line, which reached Redding, California, in 1872. Completion of the line was delayed by financial crises in the 1870s and 1880s.

In May 1887, the seemingly all-powerful Big Four assumed control of Villard's O&C. In their haste to complete the railroad over the rugged Siskiyou Mountains, the Big Four asked chief engineer William Hood to build the fastest, cheapest route over the mountains. With these instructions Hood ignored a route surveyed by O&C engineers that would have required several long tunnels and a great deal of time and expense to build. Instead he built a tortuous and steep line that featured long stretches of sustained grades in excess of 3 percent—grades significantly steeper than found on other SP lines including those over Donner Pass and in the Tehachapis. The grade over Siskiyou Summit is the steepest, highest, and longest of any on the Siskiyou Line and crosses the summit in a 3,108-foot-long tunnel at an elevation of 4,135 feet above sea level. From Siskiyou Summit the tracks drop down a long, steep grade that winds through exceptionally tight curves and several tunnels to Ashland—more than 2,200 feet lower than the summit tunnel. Tracks were joined in a classic last-spike ceremony at Ashland on December 17, 1887. Prior to this, Oregon-bound passengers were required to ride a connecting stage coach linking the two unfinished ends of the railroad. Although, slow, circuitous, and winding, through trains from the Bay Area to Portland were a vast improvement over earlier land transportation options.

In the later steam era, cab-ahead locomotives, synonymous with SP mountain operation elsewhere on the Pacific Lines, were absent from most of the Siskiyou Line. In the 1920s one of these locomotives suffered from a crown

Southern Pacific assigned many of its rebuilt SD9s to local service in Oregon. On a clear April 1990 afternoon, SD9e 4355 works Medford yard on the Siskiyou Line. *Brian Solomon*

sheet failure ascending the grade near Foliage, with catastrophic consequences.

The obvious inadequacy of SP's circuitous, steep, and sinuous Siskiyou crossing forced the railroad to investigate a better route to Oregon. Under Harriman control, SP undertook a number of bold initiatives aimed at improving its plant, operations, and service as well as coordinating operation with the Harriman-controlled Union Pacific. The Natron Cutoff started out in 1906 as a line eastward from the Eugene (Oregon) area that was intended to cross the Cascades and ultimately join the UP in eastern Oregon; Natron is located just southeast of Eugene. About the same time, SP began working its way north from Weed, California, toward Klamath Falls, Oregon, thus giving the new cutoff a two-fold purpose. Construction of these lines continued until 1912 when work was suspended because of the complicated legal battles surrounding UP and SP. In the interim, a gap of roughly 100 miles remained between the ends of track, and some of the completed line, notably tracks between Weed and Grass Lake originally built by the Weed Lumber Company, were inadequate for heavy mainline service.

More than a decade passed before work resumed, and by that time the situation had changed. The financial interests of UP and SP had been separated, and the two companies were now competing with each other for territory and business. Construction began again in September 1923, and the line was finally completed in February 1926, during which time some of the most difficult engineering projects were undertaken, notably the numerous bridges, tunnels, and snowsheds between Heather and Cascade Summit in Pengra Pass.

Although the Natron Cutoff crests at significantly higher elevation than the Siskiyou Line—4,872 feet above sea level versus just 4,135 feet—it represented a vast transportation improvement and a feat of modern engineering. Where the ruling westbound grade on the Siskiyou was an astounding 3.3 percent, the Natron Cutoff features a comparatively mild 1.8 percent climb. The new line was nearly 24 miles shorter than the old Siskiyou Route. Historian John Signor, in his book *Rails in the Shadow of Mt. Shasta,*

The Siskiyou Line received little attention or modernization after it was bypassed. As a result, some elements of operations on the line were a throwback to an earlier era—notably its traditional Union Switch & Signal lower-quadrant semaphore block signals An SP local led by SD9e 4424 splits a set of signals at Tolo, Oregon, in August 1986. *Dan Munson*

indicates that SP eliminated approximately 51 complete circles of curvature with the opening of what would become known as the Cascade Route. These improved operating conditions allowed SP to chop nearly 4½ hours from passenger schedules and operate significantly heavier freight trains. A new passenger train was introduced, appropriately named *Cascade*. Within a few months of its opening, most traffic was diverted off the Siskiyou Line to the new Cascade Route. After the Great Depression, SP gradually upgraded the line, installing CTC and lengthening sidings. By the mid 1960s, most of the Shasta Route from Roseville to Portland was controlled by CTC.

Although the Natron Cutoff diverted the majority of through freight and passenger traffic, the Siskiyou Line remained open as a through route, and passenger service remained until the 1950s. The line served the Oregon timber industry, and several freight trains originated on the Siskiyou Line until the early 1990s. In the summer of 1992, following a precipitous loss of freight originating in the area of Medford, Oregon, SP discontinued through operations over Siskiyou Summit and embargoed the line. A few years later SP sold the line to Railtex which has operated the railroad as the Central Oregon & Pacific and reopened the Siskiyou Summit crossing.

Meanwhile, Southern Pacific's Cascade crossing on the Natron Cutoff remained one of its most impressive lines and

one of the best examples of modern railroad engineering in the mountains of the West. If SP's Donner Pass has been called "railroading in a barn" in reference to the many miles of wooden snowsheds there, then SP's Cascade crossing over Pengra Pass might be called "railroading in a cloud." The weather in this region is notoriously damp, and Pacific storms will come up the valley and stall here against the mountains.

Standing near Cruzatte above Tunnel No. 6 and looking west, we look down toward the portal of tunnel No. 7. Off in the distance, two miles away (but 18 miles distant by rail), and many hundreds of feet lower, a westbound SP freight charges across the curved Salt Creek trestle at Heather, three SD45T–2s in the lead, and four. . . five . . . six SD9s cut in mid-train—moving more than 7,500 tons up grade. For more than an hour we hear the EMD's whine echoing off the mountains as they grind up through Wicopee, Fields, and Frazier. The sound fades in and out as the train passes through a dozen tunnels, numerous snowsheds, and over several tall bridges. Finally, smoke pours from the tunnel, and the train shudders out, crawling along at only 5 mph. When its helper passes, flames leap from the stacks of the SD9s, their hoods black with oil and exhaust. It's this daily struggle that makes the Oregon Cascades one of the most amazing places on the old Southern Pacific.

A set of light helpers roll downgrade through Fields, Oregon, on the Cascade Line in June 1994. *Brian Solomon*

The introduction of the *Daylight* in 1937 was a turning point for SP. The flashy new streamliner ushered in a resurgence of passenger business and in part signaled the close of the Great Depression. More *Daylight*s would follow the launching of the original San Francisco–Los Angeles train, both before and after World War II. On a clear California morning in the late 1940s, train 98, the *Morning Daylight*, rolls past Potrero Tower in San Francisco, beginning its 9-hour 45-minute run to Los Angeles. In 1940, a second San Francisco–L.A. streamliner had been added, known as the *Noon Daylight*, and the original run was renamed *Morning Daylight*. Leading the train on this day is 4459, one of only two GS-5 4-8-4s. Built in 1942, the GS-5s were nearly identical to the more common GS-4, but were slightly heavier and equipped with roller bearings. *Robert O. Hale, collection of M.D. McCarter, courtesy of Joe Welsh*

Continued from page 37

1950s it had scaled passenger operations down to just a core network and looked to be the first major American line to become strictly a freight carrier.

During the 1960s SP finally consolidated many of its traditional subsidiaries. The Texas & New Orleans and El Paso & Southwestern were merged into the parent company in 1961. Pacific Electric, which had survived as a freight carrier after the sale of passenger operations, lost its identity in 1965. During the late 1960s SP made the bold move of building an entirely new freight line at a time when other American railroads were abandoning routes: in 1967 it opened the all-new Palmdale Cutoff connecting Palmdale directly with the Sunset route at Colton, California, providing a bypass around Los Angeles for traffic to and from Northern California. In the 1960s SP considered several merger schemes. It considered dividing the Rock Island with Union Pacific, and made a bid to acquire the Western Pacific. Neither came to pass at that time.

With the coming of Amtrak in 1971, Southern Pacific was finally freed of its long-distance passenger responsibilities, allowing it to focus on freight business. However, while overall freight traffic remained robust, the company gradually lost stature and began a long decline. Mergers and acquisitions continued to be explored. Southern Pacific considered joining with Seaboard Coast Line in 1978, but SCL declined and ultimately merged with Chessie System to form CSX. Rock Island, whose routes SP eyed in the 1960s, entered bankruptcy in 1975 and was liquidated in the late 1970s. SP secured its Golden State Route connections through the acquisition of Rock Island's Tucumcari–Kansas City line in 1980. This important corridor was assigned to Cotton Belt and was known colloquially as the "Cotton Rock." By the time of SP's Rock Island acquisition, the Golden State route was suffering from years of neglect and only handling a trickle of freight traffic. In the late 1920s, after SP acquired the EP&SW, this line had been one of SP's premier gateways, at times handling more traffic than the Sunset Route east of El Paso. SP's reaffirmed commitment to the route and considerable investment in the line resulted in a gradual resurgence, and the line became a primary intermodal route during the 1980s with the development and growth of SP's double-stack business.

The early 1980s saw a flurry of railroad merger activity. In 1980, Burlington Northern acquired the Frisco—a merger that in part precipitated Union Pacific's consolidation with Missouri Pacific and Western Pacific in 1981. The later joining had serious implications for Southern Pacific. Although SP gained a significantly better St. Louis–Kansas City route by way of Missouri Pacific trackage rights, it lost a considerable share of Overland traffic to the WP route—now part of the UP system—and faced serious competition from UP in other markets. In December 1983 Southern Pacific and Santa Fe reacted to the changing Western railroad scene by combining the two companies as Southern Pacific Santa Fe, although the two railroads technically remained separate while awaiting ICC approval. Santa Fe was the dominant merger partner, and—anticipating federal approval—both roads embraced a new image and painted equipment accordingly. New image and corporate

The St. Louis Southwestern—the fabled Cotton Belt—came under SP control in the 1930s. Arguably SP's most important subsidiary, the Cotton Belt effectively brought the SP to the all-important St. Louis gateway. Though SSW adopted SP livery, its equipment retained Cotton Belt markings, as evidenced by this quartet of SSW units pourin' on the coal (or fuel oil, as the case may be) on the Sunset Route main line near Shawmut, Arizona, far from home tracks. *David P. Oroszi*

Until the Suisun Bay Bridge was completed in1930, SP ferried all of its trains headed for Oakland off the Shasta and Overland routes across the Carquinez Straits between Port Costa to Benicia, California. Led by SD40 No. 7399 clad in an experimental, retro-Daylight paint scheme, the hot OABRT (Oakland to Brooklyn Yard [Portland]) trailer train out of the Bay Area heads across the massive structure—the largest railroad bridge west of the Mississippi—on April 1, 1984. *Brian Jennison*

union notwithstanding, a combined SPSF was not to be. In July 1986 the ICC shocked the industry by rejecting SPSF on charges that it was anti-competitive. SPSF Chairman John J. Schmidt's words at the time summed up the emotionally charged situation saying, "I can assure you that virtually everyone [in the hearing room] was stunned."

SPSF appealed, but ICC refused to accept the revised merger bid. Where BN-Frisco, and UP-MP-WP were essentially end-to-end combinations, SP and Santa Fe duplicated each other in virtually every major market—a situation made suspect by the ill-fated Penn Central (Pennsylvania + New York Central) merger of 1968. SPSF was forced to dispose of SP and in 1988 the ICC approved the sale of SP to Rio Grande Industries, owned by billionaire Philip Anschutz. In the five years SP hung in the bal-

ance while its fate was decided, the railroad languished. Union with the Rio Grande had some advantages, and traffic levels improved, but SP's physical plant suffered from years of insufficient investment. Yards that had been expanded in the 1950s and 1960s were not suited to modern operations and strained with capacity problems. Southern Pacific no longer had the ability to handle its traffic efficiently.

Under Rio Grande control SP expanded into the Chicago gateway, first by the 1989 acquisition of the old Alton Railroad route between St. Louis and Joliet, Illinois, including trackage rights over Illinois Central between Joliet and Chicago, then by securing trackage rights over Burlington Northern between Kansas City and Chicago in 1990. Later, SP acquired a third route to Chicago by virtue of

continued on page 47

THE MODOC LINE

Pieced together in the late 1920s, the Modoc Line served as a shortcut for Oregon-bound traffic off the Overland Route. Hoar frost, known on the mountain as "pogonip," is just starting to clear on an icy January morning in 1993 as a Eugene-bound freight climbs toward Crest, one of several summits on the line between Wendel, California, and Klamath Falls, Oregon. *Brian Solomon*

SP's Modoc Line traverses some of the loneliest territory in the West. It skirts the far northeastern corner of California, an area nearly void of human habitation. Most of the railroad winds across open, inhospitable, windswept desert —but the sort of wide open space for which the American West is famous.

SP built the Modoc Line—sometimes called the Alturas Cutoff—as a shortcut to Oregon from the east. The line originally connected with the Overland Route at Fernley, Nevada, and from this junction cut geographically northwest through Alturas, California, to a connection with the Natron Cutoff near Klamath Falls, Oregon. The 251-mile-long railroad was 210 miles shorter than traveling via Dunsmuir, Roseville, and Donner Pass. The Modoc Line was largely assembled from existing lines, but the portion between Klamath Falls and Alturas was built new. The line opened in September 1929 less than four years after the opening of the Natron Cutoff. The two new lines effectively provided Oregon with a new transcontinental route. Passenger service was provided for the first few years but discontinued in 1937. One characteristic that distinguishes the Modoc from most other SP main lines is its lack of block signaling.

The middle section of the Modoc Line running between Wendel and Alturas is by far the most interesting. This is sinuous, grade-intensive, raw desert railroading. It was built by the Nevada-Oregon-California, a three foot-gauge railroad that pushed northward across the desert from Reno with grandiose visions of connecting Reno with the Columbia River. It reached Alturas by 1906 and Lakeview, Oregon, in 1912, but never made it any further. In 1917 the Western Pacific bought the southern portion of the N-C-O, and in 1926 Southern Pacific picked up the remainder. SP's Fernley & Lassen line from Fernley, Nevada, to Susanville, California, crossed the N-C-O at Wendel, and SP did little more than convert the narrow gauge to standard width. The line's primitive construction and winding nature is clear evidence of its narrow-gauge heritage. Climbing up out of Wendel, the railroad first ascends Viewland Hill, crosses a broad plateau, and then rises through a narrow canyon to the summit at Crest. After crossing the level Madeline Plain, the railroad climbs again to Sage Hen summit then drops down through a series of looping curves at Indian Camp and Likely before ultimately arriving at Alturas.

SP's new line connected with the N-C-O route just south of downtown Alturas, the only sizable town in the region; the remainder of the N-C-O to Lakeview was operated for many years as a branch and later sold to a shortline operator. The newly built line ascends a grueling grade from Canby—named for an American Army General massacred by the Modoc Indians—through Howards Gulch to the summit at Ambrose, and then on to Stronghold where it crosses WP's Inside Gateway, ultimately arriving at the junction with the Cascade Route near Klamath Falls at Texum.

In the steam era, the Modoc line was the last stomping ground for articulated locomotives before they were sent to scrap. As steam was gradually retired from other regions, it was sent to work on the Modoc. By the mid 1950s, it was one of the last places to witness big steam in freight service on the SP and articulateds survived here in regular service until 1956, several years after it had disappeared from most other routes.

In the early 1960s, SP acquired trackage rights from Flannagan to Winnemucca over the WP and abandoned the southern portion of the Modoc line along Pyramid Lake.

The Modoc was never a heavily traveled line. In the 1970s it hosted up to three trains per day in each direction, but in recent times normal operations saw roughly one train each way per day. In the last decade of independent SP operation, the Modoc was closed to through traffic for extended periods. Although abandonment has loomed several times, the Modoc like the proverbial Phoenix, rises again, and again. Union Pacific recently announced that the line which has been closed since 1997, has been 'railbanked' for future use.

Southern Pacific Electro-Motive SD9 5440, still wearing "black widow" paint as delivered, leads other EMDs and Alco locomotives and a southbound (eastbound by railroad timetable) freight past the Saugus, California, depot in the 1960s. "First generation" diesels such as these would soon defer to newer diesels from Electro-Motive and General Electric on mainline trains. *Herb Johnson*

Cab-Forward 4224, "in the hole" at Beaumont, California, meets a diesel-powered reefer train circa 1950. The decade-plus following World War II was the twilight of steam, not only for the SP, but for American railroads in general. Dieselization was one of the most important developmental steps in railroading. SP's pre-World War II dabblings in dieseldom led to an intensive dieselization program in the postwar era. As with virtually all other U.S. railroads, SP could not ignore the vast economic improvements that diesels could bring to operations. *T. M. Hotchkiss, Ed Crist collection*

Continued from page 44
Santa Fe trackage rights awarded as a condition of the 1995 Burlington Northern-Santa Fe merger. Although SP moved considerable traffic through its new Chicago connections, its routes were weak compared to those of Union Pacific and Santa Fe.

In the mid-1970s SP had begun to shed once-important lines and pare down its vast railway network. The San Diego & Arizona Eastern was decimated by severe washouts in 1976, and SP sold the line in 1978 to the Metropolitan Transit Development Board. Part of the line was later used for the San Diego Trolley;

In 1988, Denver billionaire Philip Anschutz bought the Southern Pacific and combined it with his Denver & Rio Grande Western. To commemorate the union, the railroads ran a special train of combined office cars from Oakland to Oregon. Although the special operated behind restored GS-4 No. 4449 in Oregon, it left the Bay Area behind freshly-scrubbed diesels of both roads. Here the train rolls east along the shores of San Pablo Bay on December 12, 1988. *Brian Jennison*

Under Rio Grande control, SP finally made its way into Chicago—the nation's rail hub. It did so first by purchasing the former Gulf, Mobile & Ohio (nee Chicago & Alton) St. Louis–Chicago line, and then by acquiring trackage rights on the Burlington Northern from Kansas City to Chicago. In the summer of 1990, an SP GP20 and a GP40 prepare to depart the old GM&O division-point yard at Bloomington, Illinois, with a westbound local. Illinois State University buildings loom in the background. SP called its former GM&O line the Southern Pacific Chicago–St. Louis (SPCSL). *Steve Smedley*

the remainder was operated for a few years by Kyle Railways. In 1980 more than a 100 miles of Rio Grande Valley trackage in Texas was discontinued in favor of trackage rights on the Missouri Pacific. SP discontinued operations on some Bay Area trackage in the mid-1980s, including the original (nee Western Pacific) line via Altamont Pass. The Northwestern Pacific north of Willits, California, to Eureka, was conveyed to shortline operator Eureka Southern which operated the line until the early 1990s. In Arizona, the Copper Basin Railroad assumed operation of SP's Hayden branch in July 1986. Less than a year later SP divested itself of a significant cluster of Louisiana branch lines centered around New Iberia to Genesee & Wyoming shortline Louisiana & Delta. Beginning in 1988, SP began selling off additional trackage to public transit agencies while retaining trackage rights—a scheme designed to cover growing operating losses. In April 1988 it sold some Dallas area trackage and two and half years later it conveyed 175 miles of L.A. Basin trackage to local authorities, some of which was later included in the Metrolink commuter-rail system. In 1993 SP identified approximately 3,000 miles of surplus and low-density lines that it wished to sell to shortlines or abandon, including its Siskiyou, Coos Bay, and Modoc lines. Although SP did not find a suitable buyer for the lightly used Modoc, it sold most of its Oregon branch lines to short-line operators including Genesee & Wyoming and RailTex, while in California it conveyed operation of three lines, including the remainder of the Northwestern Pacific, to shortline operator California Northern.

The Southern Pacific image prevailed over that of Rio Grande, and after 1992, Rio Grande and Cotton Belt names were dropped. In 1995, following the Burlington Northern-Santa Fe merger, a process disrupted by a hostile bid by Union Pacific for Santa Fe, UP announced it would purchase Southern Pacific, including Rio Grande and Cotton Belt. Shortly before the highly controversial UP-SP merger came up for review, the ICC was disbanded, and the case was heard by ICC's regulatory successor Surface Transportation Board, which approved the case while providing some concessions to competing carriers. Southern Pacific became part of Union Pacific on September 11, 1996.

Nighttime on the desk at Tower 68. In the evening hours of September 8, 1996, operator Brenda Bob watches trainee Marcus Phillips solve yet another logistical problem, one of hundreds encountered on each trick. *Tom Kline*

A loaded coal train bound for Chicago plies along the former Rio Grande Tennessee Pass (Colorado) main line near Pando in 1995. The train was part of a joint ore/coal-train operation with Wisconsin Central, and the train in this scene will return west loaded with iron ore. *Brian Solomon*

Southern Pacific passenger trains were, in their heyday, among the best in the West. The red-and-orange "Daylight" era came to be associated with the pinnacle of SP's "Friendly Service." Long after SP exited the intercity passenger business, reminders of those halcyon years exist in the form of restored SP E9 6051 and various examples of passenger rolling stock, posing at the California State Railroad Museum in 1984. *Mike Schafer and Jim Boyd*

Chapter 3

Riding the Friendly SP

Southern Pacific's Once-Extensive
Passenger Operations

Southern Pacific's passenger trains were among the most famous and best recognized in the U.S. Who hasn't heard of the *Overland*, *Sunset Limited*, *Coast Daylight*, and *Golden State*? SP's name trains defined the railroad's main lines, and former Southern Pacific routes are still known by the great passenger trains that once traversed their rails.

Southern Pacific's passenger service was atypical of Western roads. It had the largest and most developed passenger network in the far West and operated a plethora of plush named trains, secondary limiteds, mail trains, and branchline locals. It was the only carrier in the far West to operate an intensive commuter-rail network and the first railroad in the West to operate a deluxe, overnight, all-sleeping-car train. In addition to its conventional locomotive-hauled trains, Southern Pacific and its subsidiaries—notably Pacific Electric—operated the most extensive electric interurban networks in the West (see sidebar).

Southern Pacific suffered from declining ridership as early as 1914, and although ridership temporally swelled during World War I, the railroad continued to lose both long-distance and local riders during the 1920s as the automobile began its ascendancy. The railroad suffered great losses during the Great Depression, during which discretionary travel virtually dried up, resulting in a disastrous decline in ridership. In the early 1930s, new SP president Angus D. McDonald devised a plan to rejuvenate SP's sagging passenger ridership, and over a 15-year period SP made a substantial investment in its passenger services. Among the improvements was the introduction of streamlined trains. Prompted by the success of Union Pacific's M-10000 streamliner and Chicago, Burlington & Quincy's *Zephyr* 9900, both unveiled in 1934, railroads across

the land quickly joined the streamliner movement. SP was among those roads, launching its world-renown steam-powered *Daylight* streamliner in March 1937 (it had already been jointly operating the *City of San Francisco* streamliner with UP and Chicago & North Western for about a year). The *Daylight* fleet would spread.

World War II interrupted SP's passenger improvement plans, and to free equipment for military passenger moves during the war, the railroad was forced to discontinue many secondary civilian passenger trains. Southern Pacific's carefully planned passenger program and intensive advertising faced mixed results. Like most American railroads, "Espee" enjoyed enormous passenger growth during the war, but in the postwar years its ridership and passenger revenues went into decline. Although some trains were turning a profit—and advertising had successfully promoted the name trains—passenger revenues by 1950 had fallen to roughly half of those in 1945, and, save for a boom during the Korean War, ridership and revenue plummeted as the 1950s marched on.

Despite this precipitous drop in passenger ridership and revenues, SP remained fiercely loyal to its long-distance services and continued to make significant investment in its premier services. Flagship trains were maintained to the highest standards, and many regarded SP's trains among the best in the nation, if not the world. During the 1950s SP supported secondary trains on primary routes, but lesser runs that failed to draw ridership were quickly dropped. Time had run out for numerous SP branchline services, and many unnamed branch trains that had survived the Great Depression and World War II made their last runs. In 1952 SP was operating 32 named passenger trains, and as late as 1957 some premier

SP runs regularly carried up to 17 or 18 cars. Yet in that year the railroad took an abrupt turn away from its passenger business.

By the mid 1950s, automobile and airline traffic devastated SP's ridership figures, and management—particularly President D.J. Russell—felt that passengers had deserted the railroad. Despite its earlier commitment and considerable investment in new equipment, Southern Pacific adopted a draconian passenger policy. Unlike some Western roads—notably Santa Fe and UP—that continued to maintain a network of premier trains, SP began to slash schedules and decimate its famous liners. Russell's notoriously pessimistic views and negative public statements reflected a realistic assessment of public interest in the railroad's passenger service: the day of the luxury limited was coming to an end. However, his negative attitudes and public pessimism drew criticism from the media, government agencies, and passenger-train enthusiasts, and he has been condemned for dooming SP's trains. If there was a good side to all this, it was and is the belief that SP's anti-passenger stance of the 1960s was in part the catalyst for the creation of Amtrak.

The Interstate Commerce Commission was not always as sympathetic to SP's plight, sometimes insisting that SP continue operating its trains longer and more frequently than the railroad would have desired. Some historians have argued that SP drove away its passenger business by providing substandard service. One change that particularly angered passengers and railroad observers was the substitution of "Automatic Buffet Cars" for traditional railroad dining cars. By the mid-1960s, when most Western railroads were still operating classy flagship trains—Santa Fe with its *Chief*s, Union Pacific with its famous yellow-and-gray *City* streamliners, Burlington, Rio Grande, and Western Pacific with their jointly operated *California Zephyr*—Southern Pacific provided a vastly scaled down network of long-distance trains and seemed anxious to rid itself of even these. Trains that had run as full consists only a decade earlier were run as minimal consists. In 1964, the *Coast Daylight* would consist only of two Electro-Motive E-units and just six cars. Toward the very end of SP long-distance passenger service in the late 1960s, some trains were run as just a single locomotive hauling a solitary coach. Yet, although SP's late-era trains had become but spartan remnants of an earlier era known for

amenities and dedicated service, they were at least clean and well-maintained.

In 1967, SP president Benjamin F. Biaggini announced ". . .the cold fact looms that the long-distance passenger train is dead and no amount of prayer or wishful thinking can bring it back to life." Some observers felt that Espee would become the first large railroad in the U.S. to shed itself of all long-distance passenger service, but the railroad retained a core network of passenger service until May 1, 1971, when Amtrak assumed operation of most remaining American intercity passenger trains. In fact, Southern Pacific's routes became an integral part of Amtrak's network, and despite SP's negative attitude toward long-distance passenger trains, most SP main lines have hosted Amtrak trains in the nearly thirty years since SP exited the long-distance passenger business. Today, there is considerable irony that one of Amtrak's finest and most-popular trains is the *Coast Starlight*—a combination of SP's old *Cascade* and *Coast Daylight* streamliners, and that Amtrak's multi-schedule *San Joaquin* service—based in part on SP's old *San Joaquin Daylight*—is enjoying unprecedented growth and popularity. Even railroad presidents can be wrong.

PASSENGER SERVICE ON THE OVERLAND ROUTE

Central Pacific's first significant line, the original transcontinental railroad operated in conjunction with the Union Pacific (and for many years Chicago & North Western), has served as a significant passenger route since the world-famous spike ceremony at Promontory, Utah, in 1869. Lured by California in general and the San Francisco in particular, passengers have traversed the Overland Route aboard a great many named trains in the last 130 years.

Known for its precipitously steep hills, mild and pleasant climate punctuated by gentle afternoon Pacific coastal fog, its wonderfully diverse and eclectic Victorian architecture, delicious seafood and chocolate, San Francisco is one of America's favorite cities and had long been a principal destination for Southern Pacific passengers. It was a favorite subject for writers. Mark Twain, Ambrose Bierce, and the flamboyant Lucius Beebe—better known today for his many railroad books—all wrote about "The City." San Francisco was home to many important Southern Pacific personalities and the location of company headquarters

and offices. Ironically, however, although San Francisco was the destination for many SP travelers, all "San Francisco"-bound trains off the Overland and Shasta routes actually terminated in Oakland account of San Francisco's isolation on a long peninsula accessible by rail only from the south. Passengers completed their journey across San Francisco Bay to San Francisco of the way by ferry or motorcoach.

Throughout the Overland Route's years as a passenger route, the railroads—first Central Pacific, then Southern Pacific, and finally Amtrak—have continually juggled both schedules and train names operating on the route. For more than a half century, premier Overland Route runs carried the prestigious train numbers 1 and 2 as an indication of their importance to the railroad. For many years before the turn of the century, the *Atlantic Express* and *Pacific Express* trains provided transcontinental service—with a change of trains or two. The *Pacific Express* ran westbound and brought passengers within sight of its namesake ocean, but its similarly named eastbound counterpart fell far short of its

name. Passengers had a long way to go to reach the Atlantic Ocean after disembarking from the *Atlantic Express* in Council Bluffs, Iowa, but at least it got them pointed in the right direction. After 1906, the westbound train carried the even more-ambitious name *China & Japan Express*, while the eastbound was became simply known as the *Express*

Central Pacific and later SP experimented with a variety of luxury limiteds over the years. In December 1888, the *Golden Gate Special* debuted between Council Bluffs and the Bay Area. Advertised as the "The Finest Train in the World," it operated once a week with a distinctive consist of deluxe equipment decorated in the highly ornate fashion of Victorian times. Intended to attract the highest class of traveler, the train failed in its mission. It was cancelled in 1889 and its service assumed by a still fancy, but less opulent *Overland Flyer*, a train that had began running in 1887. The *Overland Limited* began service in 1896 and quickly became one of the most recognized passenger trains in America. Although it variously operated as the *Overland Limited*, *San Francisco*

The second edition of the streamliner *City of San Francisco*, introduced on January 2, 1938, is shown eastbound at Midlake, Utah, on the Lucin Cutoff. This version of the *City* initially ran once a week in each direction and was pulled by Electro-Motive's rakish E2s; note the logos of the three operating railroads on the nose of the E2A which in 1948 would become wholly owned by SP. This well-known publicity scene is believed to be a composite made from two different photographs, with the idyllic sky added separately. *SP, Tim Doherty collection*

Overland Limited, and the *San Francisco Overland*, the train was popularly known simply as the *Overland* and carried passengers from Chicago to the Bay Area. In 1902, following Harriman control of both UP and SP, the *Overland* was upgraded with the latest passenger equipment. It was one of the first trains to use steel framed cars—significantly safer and more durable than earlier all-wood designs. The rear-end, open-platform observation car featured rubber tile flooring, and the train was equipped with the latest communication innovation: the telephone.

Harriman-era improvements such as the Lucin Cutoff across the Great Salt Lake (Chapter 2) significantly shortened travel times between Ogden and Oakland. Before Harriman, a train took roughly 73 hours to make the run from Chicago to the Bay Area. Initial improvements to the railroad dropped running time by ten hours, and by the mid-1920s the *Overland* was running on an aggressive 58-hour schedule between Chicago and the Bay Area—particularly impressive considering the Overland Route was not a contiguous rail line until 1930. Prior the construction of the massive Suisin Bay Bridge—the largest double-track railroad bridge west of the Mississippi River—SP ferried its trains across Suisun Bay northeast of San Francisco, between Port Costa and Benicia, on large ferry boats. Whole trains were divided into sections and placed on ferries, then reassembled on the other side to continue their journey. For many years this was the most intensive train-ferry operation in America, and SP employed several exceptionally large ferries to perform the service. Following the opening of the Carquinez Straits Bridge and other Overland Route improvements, another two hours was chopped from the *Overland Limited*'s time.

The *Overland* was supplemented by other trains, notably the Chicago–Oakland *Gold Coast*, a middle-class, all-purpose train that tended to many stops bypassed by the more important *Overland*. Mail trains Nos. 21 and 22 and a nameless, coach-only Sparks (Nevada)–Sacramento run provided connections through to Los Angeles at Sacramento.

In 1934, Union Pacific entered the streamlined age with its articulated (sectional) streamliner, the M-10000, built by Pullman-Standard and Electro-Motive Corporation. Along with Burlington's famous *Zephyr*, this sleek aluminum-bodied, Armour-yellow train toured the nation and helped change the way the public and the railroads perceived passenger trains. Streamlined trains proved enormously popular, and within a couple of years of the debut of the M-10000 and *Zephyr*, UP, in conjunction with Chicago & North Western and Southern Pacific, introduced the Chicago-Oakland streamliner *City of San Francisco*, a train which would quickly upstage the *Overland*. Also in 1936, SP, UP, and C&NW introduced a run equipped with conventional (heavyweight) air-conditioned luxury equipment called the *San Francisco Challenger*.

Initially, the *City of San Francisco* was operated with a single set of equipment and thus could provide only five "sailings" per month—about every six days—from each terminal. Not only was it the first streamliner on the SP, but the first diesel-power mainline train. The popularity of the *City* soon dictated additional new trainsets in 1937–38 which allowed for greater service frequency. Also in 1937, UP, SP, and C&NW inaugurated the *Forty-Niner*, a steam-powered, all-sleeping-car train comprised largely of rebuilt, semi-streamlined rolling stock. In 1939, the mostly heavyweight *Treasure Island Special* was added for two years to accommodate travelers heading for the World's Fair at San Francisco.

But 1939 was also a low point for the Overland Route. On August 12 of that year, saboteurs sent the middle cars of the *City of San Francisco* careening off a bridge over a dry wash in a particularly remote area of Nevada, killing several passengers and crew members. The F.B.I. put out an all-points bulletin for the perpetrator(s), but they were never found and the mystery remains unsolved to this day.

Additional new UP and SP streamlined cars were delivered in 1941 just before war restrictions were placed on the nation's railroads. The new cars allowed for yet another increase in the *City*'s service frequency. In addition, some cars from this latest delivery were used to bolster *San Francisco Overland* trains.

The postwar era brought several changes to SP's Overland Route. Like many other railroads, SP had high hopes for continued prosperity in the passenger department. Toward this end, SP and Overland Route partners UP and C&NW ordered much new rolling stock for their entire passenger-train networks. New cars allowed the *City of San Francisco* to finally go daily in 1947, although the *San Francisco Challenger* was discontinued that same year. In 1951, the *San Francisco Overland* was completely streamlined. In fact, for several years thereafter, the *San Francisco Overland* served as a true transcontinental service, carrying through sleepers for both New York City and Washington D.C. Though still overshadowed by its more famous counterpart—the *City of San Francisco*—the *San Francisco Overland* had nothing to apologize for. The *Overland*'s schedule provided riders with daylight views of the Sierras, which the *City of San Francisco* traversed largely in hours of darkness. Further, the *San Francisco Overland* would be the first SP train to get a dome car, in 1954.

The precipitous nationwide decline in rail passenger ridership during the 1950s was felt on the Overland Route as well as everywhere else. This decade would see the end of the *Gold Coast* and other secondary Overland trains. By 1956, the *San Francisco Overland* had evolved into little more than a connection train to the UP-Wabash *City of St. Louis* at Ogden. Finally, in 1962 the *San Francisco Overland* was "combined" with the *City of San Francisco*, effectively losing its identity.

As a survivor, the *City* remained relatively strong into the 1960s, but in 1970 its frequency reverted to tri-weekly. When Amtrak assumed most intercity passenger operations on May 1, 1971, the *City* came under the new carrier's wing and daily service eventually was restored. Briefly named *California Zephyr*, the train was renamed *San Francisco Zephyr* in November 1971. Under Amtrak the run had, by default, become the nation's sole-surviving Chicago–Bay Area passenger train! In 1983 the train was rechristened *California Zephyr* and rerouted off the UP and SP between Denver, Ogden, and Alazon, Nevada, when it was shifted to Rio Grande's Moffat Tunnel Route via Salt Lake City and UP's former WP line west of Salt Lake to Alazon. Regardless, by the end of the twentieth century, rail passengers were still being thrilled by spectacular views of Donner Pass.

PASSENGER SERVICE ON THE COAST LINE AND SAN JOAQUIN VALLEY ROUTE

Two SP main lines linked the Bay Area and Los Angeles. The San Joaquin Route via Bakersfield was completed in 1876, and the Coast Line opened in 1901 via San Luis Obispo. The Coast Line's 470-mile route between California's two largest cities—for many years the two most significant population centers on the West Coast—was one of SP's premier passenger corridors and certainly one of the most

Late in the evening at Los Angeles Union Passenger Terminal in the late 1940s, overnight passenger trains prepare for departure. In the foreground, GS-4 4451 in *Daylight* paint waits at platform 6 with train 69, the *Coaster*, a secondary coach-and-sleeper overnighter between Los Angeles and San Francisco. In 1949, this train would be renumbered and renamed *Starlight*. In the background, the head-end cars of the all-Pullman *Lark* get a workover prior to the train's departure about an hour after the *Coaster*. Robert O. Hale, collection of M.D. McCarter, courtesy of Joe M. Welsh

© STANLEY A. PILTZ

2B-H322

With their red, orange, and black livery, impressive Northern-type locomotives that were not too overdone in the streamlining department, and a wonderfully scenic route, SP's Coast Line Daylights were nearly the perfect passenger trains. Mike Schafer collection

intensive long-distance corridors in the West. Known as "Route of a Thousand Wonders," the scenery was spectacular. Where else could you gaze out over the Pacific Ocean for more than 100 miles while dining on board a train?

Soon after the Coast Line open to through service, Southern Pacific introduced the aptly named *Coast Line Limited*. In 1906 it was replaced by a new train called the *Coaster*. During this early period SP also operated a deluxe, all-parlor-car train called the *Shore Line Limited* that sprinted between San Francisco and Los Angeles in just 13 1/2 hours—a remarkably fast schedule for the period.

Overnight trains were very popular in the days before air travel, and in May 1910, at its Arcade Street Station in Los Angeles, Southern Pacific debuted its first and most famous night train, the *Lark*, an exclusive all-Pullman train to and from downtown San Francisco. Heralded as the first all-sleeping car train in the West, the *Lark* was compared to New York Central's famous *20th Century Limited* and aimed at businessmen traveling between California's two largest cities. It was electrically lighted and offered deluxe accommodations.

In its first few years the train often ran with seven wood cars—typical of the era—hauled by one of SP's high-driver 4-4-2 Atlantics. By the late 1920s when the *Lark* had acquired elite status and was popular with Hollywood movie stars as well as business clientele, it was running with 9 or 10 cars—by now all-steel and hauled by a 4-6-2 Pacific or a 4-8-2 Mountain type. In the 1930s, it was making its run in

under 14 hours, regularly carrying 11 through cars between San Francisco and Los Angeles Beginning in 1931, when the overnight Oakland–Los Angeles *Padre* was discontinued, the *Lark* acquired an Oakland section that was joined to or split from the main section of the train at San Jose. Meanwhile, overnight coach service was provided the *Coaster*, which also carried standard sleeping cars.

In 1922, Southern Pacific inaugurated the weekend-only *Daylight Limited* between San Francisco and Los Angeles over the Coast Line. The train made no revenue stops between the terminals and featured a uniquely designed open-end observation car in which the last two-thirds of the car were open air. In addition, lunch-counter coaches provided a drugstore-counterlike service advertised as "All-Day Lunch Cars." By late summer 1923 the *Daylight Limited* had become a daily operation. This train with its simple name, to distinguish it from popular overnight limiteds, likely would have been lost in the ledgers of SP's lessor-known limiteds had it not been selected for an especially significant service upgrade in the mid-1930s.

Alarmed by the precipitous drop in passenger train ridership in the early 1930s, SP management hired a consulting firm to make service improvement recommendations. Planning began in 1933, and SP initially considered an internal-combustion-powered streamliner similar to Burlington's famous *Zephyr* and Union Pacific's M-10000. However, following the recommendations of President Angus McDonald and others, SP instead chose more conventional technology, ordering streamlined 4-8-4s from Lima Locomotive Works and a fleet of modern lightweight passenger cars from Pullman-Standard. In 1937 SP debuted its new *Daylight*, splendidly dressed in a bright, distinctive paint scheme that elegantly blended orange, red, and black. Locomotives were painted to match the cars and incorporated brilliant silver accenting the train's other colors. At a time when locomotives were typically painted black, and passenger equipment was routinely a utilitarian Pullman green, the new *Daylight* stood out among all other trains.

The distinctive paint scheme associated with the *Daylight* has come to take its name, and the handsome Lima 4-8-4s were universally known as "Daylights" regardless of the service they worked. The original *Daylight* train consisted of 12 cars, with seats for 449 passengers, and initially made its run in just 9³/₄ hours, more than two hours faster than the old *Daylight Limited*. As the train matured, the time was trimmed, and by the early 1940s, it did the run in just 9¹/₂ hours. Every morning the *Daylight*s left Los Angeles and San Francisco at 8:15 a.m., breezing passengers along SP's spectacularly scenic Coast Line and getting them to their destinations in time for a leisurely post-trip dinner.

Like other new streamliners around the nation, the *Daylight* was enormously successful and its great popularity spurred a whole family of *Daylight* trains. In the early 1940s, California was already internationally known for its automobile society, yet the *Daylight* was experiencing record-making patronage. People adored the flashy, colorful streamliner, and to accommodate overflow passengers, SP was compelled to run extra sections of the train using conventional equipment. The *Daylight* passed through several name changes. In January 1940 SP introduced a companion *Noon Daylight* using the original equipment, and the original *Daylight* runs were renamed *Morning Daylight* using new, 14-car streamlined consists. Later, as more *Daylight*s were introduced on other routes, the *Noon Daylight* was renamed the *Coast Daylight* to distinguish it

Train 99, the northbound *Morning Daylight*, steams out of Los Angeles on December 16, 1945, en route to San Francisco behind GS-series 4-8-4 No. 4432. *Photo, H. L. Kelso, Ed Crist collection; postcard, Mike Schafer collection*

from its brethren which served various parts of the SP system.

In 1941, the *San Joaquin*—the primary Oakland–Los Angeles day train via Fresno, the San Joaquin Valley, and Bakersfield—was transformed into the *San Joaquin Daylight* as new streamlined cars were placed into service on the inland route. During World War II, the scope of the *Daylight* trains was somewhat curtailed, but a full complement of trains resumed after hostilities. Following World War II, SP added to the family of trains the *Sacramento Daylight*, which ran from Sacramento to Lathrop where it connected with the *San Joaquin Daylight*. To power the *Daylight*s, SP assembled an impressive fleet of locomotives, one of the largest rosters of streamlined steam in the U.S.

The *Daylight*s had fulfilled the ambitions and visions of Angus McDonald and were duly promoted for their comfort and toted as "the most beautiful trains in the world." Who could argue? The sight of a Lima 4-8-4 whisking a 12-car streamlined *Daylight* along coastal bluffs against a backdrop of pounding Pacific surf could inspire the travel bug in even the most pedestrian Californian. Extra-large windows afforded passengers an exceptional view of the Pacific Coast, and reclining chairs offered an

unusually comfortable ride. Streamlined *Daylight*s presented the zenith of Espee passenger service, and it's hard to believe that passengers would later forsake such luxury for the confines of Boeing 707s or a tedious, eight-hour death march in an automobile on "the 101."

Following the enormous success of the new streamlined *Daylight*, Southern Pacific decided to similarly re-equip the *Lark*, and on July 10, 1941, SP debuted the new streamlined *Lark* as a modern overnight companion to the *Daylight*. Interestingly, rather than adopt the red/orange/black livery for all its streamliners, SP painted the new *Lark* equipment in a sleek, two-tone gray scheme. The interior featured modern Art Deco design with stylish engraved illuminated glass panels, soft fluorescent lighting, and pastel colors. Its most stunning and unique feature was the 200-plus-foot-long, three-section articulated "Lark Club." This elegant, sophisticated car featured a kitchen-dormitory, a dining area, and a half-moon bar and lounge section. The space flexibility of the exceptionally long Lark Club allowed SP to seat 24 people for dinner and 56 for breakfast. (Patrons were fairly leisurely about the time they had dinner, allowing SP several hours to serve everyone aboard the train, but in the morning people were hurried to eat breakfast

The *San Joaquin Daylight*, train No. 52, departs the "Oakland Mole" (Oakland Pier) depot behind GS-4 4448. The large train shed at Oakland was one of the few arched sheds on the West Coast. From this point passengers could catch ferries to San Francisco. SP served two depots in Oakland, the Mole and 16th Street four miles north. *Robert O. Hale, collection of M.D. McCarter, courtesy of Joe Welsh*

before the train arrived at its terminal.) The doors of the Lark Club were electro-pneumatically operated, and the windows covered with venetian blinds. SP paid $247,000 for the Lark Club, a princely sum for a new passenger car in the early 1940s.

Southern Pacific advertised "It's Smart to Ride the *Lark*!" and promoted the train along with the *Daylight*s as "One of the most beauti-

ful trains in America." Still focusing on the lucrative business trade, SP continued to improve the train in an effort to make it more appealing to business travelers. For many years the trains left their respective terminals at about 9 p.m. and arrived at 9 a.m thus giving riders a full night's sleep, with time for a late dinner, relaxation, perhaps a little paperwork, and breakfast. In 1949, the "Lark Phone" was

What could be more inviting than to pass through these gates at SP's Third and Townsend depot in San Francisco to catch the streamlined *Daylight*. *Joe Welsh collection*

One of the attractions of the streamlined *Lark*—sometimes called the "Night Daylight"—was its articulated Lark Club. An SP publicity photo from the World War II period makes traveling on the *Lark* look particularly appealing to businessmen, especially those in search of an attractive date. Note, too, the *Lark* monograms on the tablecloths. *Tim Doherty collection*

SP was one of the few railroads to simultaneously employ two different passenger-train paint schemes to its trains. In the early years of SP streamliners, the overnight trains carried a two-tone gray livery as illustrated by this observation-car view of the *Lark*, the premier overnighter between the Bay Area and Los Angeles. *Robert O. Hale, collection of M.D. McCarter, courtesy of Joe Welsh*

installed on the Lark Club—a state-of-the art radio telephone. "You can call from the Lark Club to any phone, anywhere in the world (even on the other *Lark*) while the train is in full flight." The service was considered remarkable in an era long before personal cell phones and direct international dialing. How many business clients were awed from a crackling call from a colleague phoning from a train cruising along the coast?

The *Lark*'s buffet-lounge observation car and a number of sleepers just ahead of it operated separate from the main section of the train between San Jose and Oakland as the *Oakland Lark*. The buffet section of the observation car provided a light breakfast for Oakland-bound travelers.

In the late steam era the *Lark* was hauled by the same streamlined 4-8-4s that were assigned to *Daylight* trains. After steam was bumped to less glamorous assignments, Alco PA diesel-electrics and, later, EMD E-units hauled the *Lark*. The streamlined *Lark* often ran with 18 cars, and it wasn't unusual for it to have as many as 21 cars. In the late 1940s, it regularly carried about 250 passengers, yet had capacity for as many as 320. The *Lark*'s consists remained heavy into the mid-1950s, even when other trains were suffering from lack of ridership. In 1957, the train lost its all-Pullman status when it began carrying coaches following the *Lark*'s combining with the *Starlight*— the streamlined overnight coach train. The *Starlight* was in fact the old *Coaster* run, which in 1949 had been renamed and streamlined using the 1937 *Daylight* equipment. In 1960, the *Oakland Lark* was dropped.

The *Lark* was the subject of great political and public controversy in the mid-1960s when SP attempted to discontinue the train. Although initially foiled, in 1968 the railroad finally got permission to kill the train and the *Lark* faded into history. By the time this legendary train ran its last miles, the majority of business travelers were using jet planes, and although direct long-distance passenger service between San Francisco and Los Angeles survived a few more years, it was never the same. The *Coast Daylight* remained the sole train on the route after the *Lark* vanished, and its operation was assumed by Amtrak in 1971 which moved the train to Oakland and combined it with what had been the old *Cascade*, emerging as the *Coast Starlight*. For a brief period in the 1980s, Amtrak revived overnight Bay Area-L.A. service with the state-supported *Spirit of California*, but it didn't catch on.

One more Coast Line train deserves mention. One of the last intercity passenger trains to serve SP's handsome Spanish Revival-style terminal at Third and Townsend streets in San Francisco was—along with the *Coast Daylight*—the *Del Monte*, which ran via the Coast Line and Monterey branch to Monterey and in earlier years all the way to Pacific Grove. In its final years only two cars long (but featuring parlor and lounge service), this train was a survivor that had experienced many name and terminal changes in its long history. But like so many trains, it vanished with the coming of Amtrak.

On the San Joaquin Route, the *San Joaquin Daylight* and its *Sacramento Daylight* connection

By the time this scene of the northbound *Coast Daylight* leaving Los Angeles was recorded on November 21, 1964, SP had pretty much given up on passenger trains. This day's train has but five cars, including a dome-lounge, coffee-shop diner, and parlor car; absent is the parlor-observation car. A "black widow"-scheme F-unit leads the abbreviated train. *Joe McMillan*

61

The scenic highlight of the *San Joaquin Daylight*'s run was traversing famous Tehachapi Loop at Walong, near Keene, California. Train 51, bound for Oakland, passes Walong on February 7, 1970. Even in its last days, this train retained its round-end observation car. SP had long since dispensed with traditional red, orange, and black *Daylight* livery, opting instead to remove the fluting from its Pullman-Standard *Daylight* cars (to reduce rust problems) and repaint them silver with a red letterboard. *Joe McMillan*

remained the premier day train, lasting up until Amtrak. During the steam era, a nameless all-coach local operating on a near-24-hour schedule served the line. Two overnight trains—the Oakland–L.A. *Owl* and the Portland–Sacramento–L.A. *West Coast*—operated within minutes of each other in both directions south of Lathrop. San Joaquin Valley service vanished with the coming of Amtrak, but in 1974 Amtrak and the State of California restored service between Oakland and Bakersfield, partially along SP lines, and it has been growing ever since.

SHASTA ROUTE SERVICE

Direct passenger service from the Bay Area to Oregon commenced shortly after the completion of the Siskiyou Line via Grants Pass, Oregon, in 1887, with the introduction of the *Oregon Express* northward (railroad timetable east) and *California Express* southward (railroad timetable west). Southern Pacific promoted the line, taking advantage of the stunning views it offered of Mt. Shasta, a dormant volcano looming more than 14,000 feet above sea level and visible from 100 miles distant. SP's *Shasta Express* began service in 1901 and was later introduced as the *Shasta Limited*. In addition to through service, SP promoted tourism in the Sacramento River valley, which the Shasta Route shared from Sacramento north to the Mt. Shasta area—long a popular holiday destination.

North of Dunsmuir, California, the twisting, winding, grade-intensive Siskiyou Line was not conducive to fast running, and passenger train service over the route was tedious and

slow. The earliest express trains were allowed 42 hours from Oakland to Portland. By 1893, the schedule had been tightened up somewhat, but it still took 36 hours for a train to make it from 16th Street Station in Oakland to Portland. Nearly 24 hours were allowed just for the run between Dunsmuir and Portland.

The Siskiyou Line was the site of one of the last classic train robberies. On October 11, 1923, at the east portal of the summit tunnel at the top of the Siskiyou grade, two bandits, brothers Hugh and Roy DeAutremont, leapt aboard train No. 13, a section of the *San Francisco Express*. They forced their way into the locomotive and demanded the engineer stop the train at the west end of the tunnel where another brother, Ray, was waiting with dynamite. There they attempted to retrieve money stored in a baggage car safe by blowing it up, but only succeeded in destroying the safe and its contents along with the baggage car and its attendant, who was killed in the explosion. Foiled by their stupidity and frustrated with

Cab-Forward 4120, a Class AC-5 built by Baldwin in 1929, and its all-heavyweight *West Coast*, train 60, greets the bright morning sun at Newhall, California, just north (timetable west) of Los Angeles circa 1950. The *West Coast* was a Portland–Los Angeles run via Sacramento, operating overnight between Sacramento and L.A. along with the Oakland–L.A. *Owl. Donald Duke, Ed Crist collection*

the botched robbery, the three brothers murdered surviving members of the train crew and rode off. Years later they were caught and sentenced to prison.

Inadequacies with the Siskiyou Line led SP to seek a more efficient route to Oregon, and in 1926, after years of construction, the Natron Cutoff via Cascade Summit opened for service. This greatly speeded up passenger operations, and Oakland-Portland schedules were trimmed by as much as 4.5 hours. To promote the new route, SP introduced a new train called the *Cascade* which for many years carried Seattle-bound through sleeping cars. In 1950, Southern Pacific upgraded the *Cascade* to a diesel-powered streamlined consist. That same year, the railroad debuted the latest and the last member of its *Daylight* fleet: the exotic *Shasta Daylight*. This diesel-powered, 15-car streamliner made the 718-mile Oakland-Portland run in under 16 hours, nearly three hours faster than earlier schedules and a vast improvement over the 42-hour schedule of the Siskiyou Line trains 63 years earlier. The *Shasta Daylight* was one of the few SP passenger trains to feature one of SP's homebuilt dome lounges. Views of the 14,161-foot-tall Mt. Shasta from the *Shasta Daylight*'s three-quarter-length dome section were one of the selling features of this popular train. Ironically, the *Shasta Daylight* was among the early victims of SP's new, draconian passenger policy, first being reduced to a tri-weekly schedule during the off-travel season in 1959, then to a summer-only train in 1964, and finally discontinued altogether in 1967.

In addition to its better-known trains, SP offered a variety of other services on the Shasta Route over the years. For several years the *West Coast* provided direct service from Portland to Los Angeles via Sacramento and the San Joaquin Valley. After 1949, the train only operated between Sacramento and L.A. The *Klamath* provided overnight service on the Shasta Route between Oakland and Portland on a more relaxed schedule then the streamliners. In 1955 it departed Oakland's 16th Street Station at 8:20 P.M. and arrived in Portland at 7:55 P.M. the following evening. Unlike the *Shasta Daylight* and *Cascade* streamliners, the *Klamath* made numerous local stops, pausing for passengers at the likes of Red Bluff, Black Butte, and Dorris, California, among other lesser-known spots. Although most passenger traffic was shifted to the Cascade Line after the Natron Cutoff opened in 1926, passenger

Scenic dayliner of SP's breathtaking Shasta Route was the *Shasta Daylight*, the last official streamliner that Espee launched, in 1950. The train was diesel-powered from the start and was usually assigned Alco PAs as depicted in this promotional artwork from the period. *Joe Welsh collection*

"The million dollar train with the million dollar view"... *Shasta Daylight* service remained on the Siskiyou Line in the form of an all-stops run known as the *Rogue River* running daily between Portland and Ashland, Oregon, into the 1950s.

PASSENGER TRAINS OF THE SUNSET AND GOLDEN STATE ROUTES

Symbolizing our nation's westward thrust and the SP's California origins, the golden setting sun over glistening rails running to the horizon is the most indelible symbol of the Southern Pacific. SP historians Neill C. Wilson and Frank J. Taylor credit the origin of this famous herald to a Texas & New Orleans employee named N. R. Olcott, who is said to have sketched it in 1876. The Southern Pacific adapted the sunset logo in dozens of ways over the years, and toward the end of its independence reintroduced a modern version of the logo on company documents and equipment. When SP adopted the Sunset Route name is unclear. By 1892—two years prior the introduction of its namesake limited—the Sunset Route was being touted in promotional literature.

Southern Pacific introduced the *Sunset Limited* in 1894 as a weekly Pullman train between San Francisco and New Orleans via Los Angeles. Advertised as the "Quickest, Safest and [most] pleasant route to the Coast," the train quickly grew in popularity and was operated more frequently as demand grew. Although operated variously as the *Sunset Limited* and *Sunset Express*, by the advent of World War I in Europe, the *Sunset Limited* was operating on a daily schedule. In 1936 the train was assigned premier train numbers 1 westbound, and 2 eastbound, identification it

retains to this day, even under the Amtrak banner. Through service to San Francisco via the Coast Line ended during World War II, and Los Angeles Union Passenger Terminal become the train's westernmost terminal.

Curiously, SP was slow to modernize the *Sunset Limited*. While new trains were rolling around the system showing off sleek streamlined profiles, the solid old *Sunset* retained its traditional heavyweight consist.

Finally, following the rigors and strains of World War II, which left the heavily used train tired and worse for the wear, SP ordered new Electro-Motive E7 passenger diesels and enough new cars from the Budd Company to re-equip five *Sunset* consists, and the venerable train finally achieved streamliner status in 1950 on a new, faster schedule—just 42 hours between Los Angeles and New Orleans.

In its twilight years as a Southern Pacific train, the *Sunset* was reduced from daily to tri-weekly and stripped of its amenities, including sleepers, lounge, and full diner; food instead was served from vending machines. So great was the resulting public outcry that the Interstate Commerce Commission was compelled to force SP to reinstate sleeper, diner, and lounge services in 1970 and maintain some basic service standards. Amtrak inherited the train in 1971, and today the *Sunset Limited* is one of the few trains operated by the national passenger carrier that retains its traditional name. Now carrying a full complement of modern bilevel sleeping cars, coaches, diner, and Sightseer Lounge, today's *Sunset Limited* has been

In the late 1940s and early 1950s Southern Pacific made a concerted effort to improve its passenger services and introduced a host of new streamlined trains, including a new Sunset Limited linking Los Angeles and New Orleans. Despite Alco PAs being depicted on this brochure announcing the 1950 edition of the Sunset, the train was usually assigned Electro-Motive locomotives. *Joe Welsh collection*

Following its overnight trek from Los Angeles, Southern Pacific No. 2, the eastbound *Sunset*, pauses at Phoenix, Arizona, on Nov. 2, 1968. An F-unit and E-unit are in charge of the train on this day. In the background are the cars for Santa Fe's Williams Junction–Phoenix run. *Joe McMillan*

extended to Florida making it the nation's first true transcontinental passenger train.

The *Sunset Limited* is by far the route's best-known train, but it was not the only passenger run on the Sunset Route. In addition to the *Golden State Limited* (see following), the Sunset Route also hosted the Los Angeles–New Orleans *Argonaut*, the New Orleans–Houston *Acadian*, the Los Angeles–Chicago *Imperial*, and the short-lived (1940–42) Chicago–Phoenix *Arizona Limited*. In the 1930s Southern Pacific proposed a diesel-electric streamliner called the *Robert E. Lee* that was to have run on a 59-hour schedule from New York to Los Angeles by way of Atlanta in conjunction with the Southern Railway, but it never made it beyond the drawing board.

The Golden State Route was essentially a branch off the Sunset Route at El Paso, Texas, extending northeast 332 miles to Tucumcari, New Mexico, where it met the Rock Island. Southern Pacific began handling the Los Angeles–El Paso portion of the Los Angeles–Chicago *Golden State Limited* in 1902, and after 1924 (when SP acquired the El Paso & Southwest-

ern) it operated the train all the way to Tucumcari from which Rock Island (and for a time, also Chicago & Alton) forwarded it to Chicago. The train provided direct competition to the roughly parallel Santa Fe. By the 1920s the train was regularly running with a fleet of handsome, heavyweight all-steel cars. In heavy periods it would rate ten Pullmans, some terminating at distant cities on various points on the Rock Island. Passengers could ride directly from Minneapolis, Des Moines, and Memphis to Los Angeles on the *Golden State Limited*.

The *Golden State Limited* was one of Rock Island's premier trains. It gave the railroad a through connection to the West, symbolically important to the company, the Chicago, Rock Island & Pacific—one of several ambitious Midwestern railroads whose tracks never directly reached the Pacific Coast. Yet, the train had a sort of secondary status on SP after its glory years in the 1920s. Southern Pacific deferred its energies to other trains and other routes and let the *GSL* languish—to the frustration of Rock Island management. Rock Island pressed SP for service improvements in

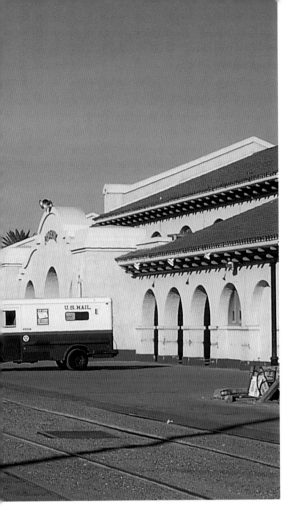

the 1930s and 1940s, but SP stalled. In the streamliner era, Rock Island had grand visions of launching a Chicago–Los Angeles streamliner dubbed the *Golden Rocket*. It would have fit in nicely with its other flashy *Rocket*s, but the train never made it past conceptualization, although some rolling stock was delivered. Instead, Rock Island and SP introduced a streamlined *Golden State* (the "*Limited*" was dropped at this time) in 1947. The train was assigned new Electro-Motive E7s painted in vermilion and silver, and as such was the first SP passenger train to regularly used diesel-electric locomotives out of the L.A. Basin. The train survived for 21 more years when in 1968 the *Golden State* was discontinued .

SP's Sunset Route also included a number of lines in Texas that connected to the L.A.–New Orleans main line. Notable among these was the Dallas–Houston corridor, operated under the auspices of SP subsidiary Texas & New Orleans. This route was served by the *Sunbeam* and the overnight *Owl* (not to be confused with the Oakland–L.A. overnight train of the same name). The streamlined *Sunbeam* entered service only a few months after

its flashy cousin streamliner, the *Daylight*, was unveiled. Although overshadowed by its more well-known cousin, the *Sunbeam* was very much a flashy train, complete with coaches, parlor, and diner-observation-lounge, all resplendent in the new orange, red, and black *Daylight* colors. Each of the two *Sunbeam* trainsets made one daily round trip on the 264-mile route, providing morning and afternoon service in each direction. Eventually, the morning runs were renamed *Hustler*. By the end of 1955, the two streamliners were gone, and by the 1960s so was the *Owl*. For a brief time in the 1990s, Amtrak instituted passenger service over much of the SP's Dallas–Houston route when it added a Houston leg to the Chicago–San Antonio *Texas Eagle*. Alas, budgetary problems resulted in the run's premature demise.

PENINSULA COMMUTES

Where other railroads ran suburban service or commuter trains, SP operated "commutes." The most intensive non-electrified passenger rail service west of Chicago was SP's San Francisco–San Jose commute service. The trains were primarily designed to deliver passengers to San Francisco in the morning and shuffle them home again at night. Commuter business was initially shunned by the nation's railroads, but ultimately they warmed to the idea. By the 1890s railroad commuting was big business on the East Coast where vast networks of lines grew up around Boston, New York, and Philadelphia. Commuter rail also became popular in the Midwest in Chicago.

Southern Pacific began to develop its Peninsula commute line in the 1890s. E. H. Harriman made a strong commitment to the line by building the Bayshore Cutoff, a 10-mile line begun in 1904 and completed roughly two years later that greatly improved SP's access to San Francisco from the south. Using a network of long fills, cuts, and several tunnels, the cutoff greatly shortened the route into the city, eliminated several grades and long stretches of street running, and double-tracked the line. A provision was made for additional tracks on the new cutoff, and SP even considered electrifying the line in the manner of the New Haven and Pennsylvania Railroad suburban electrification schemes of the same period. The commutes were up to 24 weekday round trips during the 1920s.

In the mid-1950s SP's San Francisco commute parade caught notice because it was

SP's Suburban Electric Lines

Southern Pacific's vast railway operations encompassed four different West Coast suburban networks. The oldest, most diverse, and by far the largest, longest-lived, and best-remembered of these was the famous Pacific Electric. Largely the brainchild of C. P. Huntington's nephew Henry E. Huntington, who began dabbling with Los Angeles electric railways in 1898, Pacific Electric grew into the most extensive, comprehensive, and elaborate interurban electric system ever assembled and was duly promoted as "the world's greatest interurban railway." At its peak the PE operated more than 3,200 cars over 62 routes comprised of roughly 1,260 track-miles. Running from the mountains to the Pacific and from downtown to the orange groves, PE connected Los Angeles with nearly every surrounding community including Pasadena, Long Beach, Santa Ana, Hollywood, Santa Monica, and Glendale. The railway's growth paralleled the rapid expansion of Southern California in the early twentieth century and PE's big red cars were a symbol of Los Angeles' prosperity. Though by far an electric operation, PE also fielded limited steam and diesel operations in selected freight services.

Although PE's dismantlement began gradually in the late 1920s, some routes carried passengers until 1961, and a few ex-PE lines still host (diesel) freight operations. The abandonment of PE's extensive rail-transit operations was steeped in controversy account of having been acquired, in the late 1950s by a bus operator backed by highway interests. But electric railway proponents were vindicated as L.A. began rebuilding its rail-transit system in the 1990s—some of it over previously abandoned PE rights-of-way.

SP also had suburban/interurban operations in California's second-largest metro region, the Bay Area. In 1911 Southern Pacific electrified a number of its East Bay routes—lines radiating some 40 miles from Oakland, serving Berkeley, Alameda, and San Leandro. Steel, owl-eyed electric cars plied the streets and alleys of the East Bay bringing commuters to the ferries in Oakland for the ride over to San Francisco. The system suffered terrible traffic losses with the completion of the Oakland Bay Bridge in 1936. SP electric cars began to use the lower deck of the famous bridge in 1939, but it was too late. The service couldn't compete effectively and ended just two years later. East Bay's Key System, a competing electric railway, took over some SP routes and operated across the bridge until 1957. Oakland's 16th Street Station featured an upper level for the SP electric cars, and more than 50 years after electric service ended, the upper-level platforms and canopies remained as a stark reminder to the convenience once afforded by SP's red electrics.

Perhaps the most curious of SP's electric systems was the third-rail electric operation of its Northwestern Pacific subsidiary in Marin County, north of San Francisco. The electrification began in 1903 under the operation of the North Shore Railroad (no relation to Samuel Insull's famous Chicago North Shore & Milwaukee interurban). Several routes connected Fairfax, San Rafael, and Mill Valley with a ferry terminal at Sausalito. The system was well-patronized in its early years, but ridership was devastated with the completion of the Golden Gate Bridge which offered automobiles and buses a direct route from Marin County to San Francisco. Like the East Bay overhead electric system, the NWP electric lines were discontinued in 1941.

The last electric system that Southern Pacific built and the first that it abandoned was the Oregon Electric line serving Portland and the Willamette Valley. When new in 1912, OE was the epitome of a modern electric railway and was among the first lines to use all-steel interurban cars. Yet, it was relatively short-lived, and SP abandoned it in 1929 transferring its still reasonably new cars to its other electrified lines.

The Pacific Electric was a Southern California institution for more than half a century. For thousands of folks in the L.A. Basin, PE's red cars, one of which is shown plying the streets of L.A. in 1957, provided comfortable, non-polluting, reliable transportation to hundreds of places. In the 1988 hit movie "Who Framed Roger Rabbit?" the PE—or, more to the point, it's controversial demise—was obliquely featured as a political statement. *John Dziobko*

among the last great steam shows left in the West. When new diesels bumped SP premier passenger steam from named passenger trains, these locomotives were assigned to commute service. In the afternoon, high-driver Pacifics could be found alongside Mountains and SP's legendary Lima-built Northerns—albeit sans their elaborate shrouding and fancy paint—at Third and Townsend in San Francisco waiting to lead the afternoon parade down the peninsula. These grand machines no longer rated the best runs, but they were given one last blast before they were finally sent to scrap.

Following the demise of steam, SP began using its fleet of Fairbanks-Morse Train Masters on the Peninsula trains along with steam-generator-equipped GP9s. The Train Masters survived in commute service until the mid-1970s, making them one of the last such fleets operated by a Class I railroad. In 1973 SP's fleet of 20-cylinder SDP45s—bumped from long-distance passenger duties—began to replace the F-Ms.

In 1955 the railroad began supplementing its aging heavyweight commuter coach fleet with 46 new "gallery"-style double-deck cars from Pullman-Standard. Each car was 15 feet 8 inches tall, 85 feet long, and had seats for 145 passengers—a dramatic increase over the older equipment.

Southern Pacific continued to run its commute trains for nearly a decade after Amtrak assumed operation of the railroad's long-distance services in May 1971. Yet by the early 1980s, privately operated commuter services had also become a thing of the past, and SP's commutes were one of the last privately operated suburban networks in the U.S. Caltrans—California's Department of Transportation agency—assumed financial responsibility for the San Francisco–San Jose commutes in 1980 (calling them "CalTrains"), although SP remained as a contract operator for another decade. A more distinct visual change occurred in 1985 when the State of California bought a fleet of new Japanese-built, double-deck push-pull cars and 18 Electro-Motive F40PH diesel-electrics. The last of SP's equipment, including its fleet of passenger cars, some of which dated to the Harriman era, was retired from the service in 1986. Peninsula commute service has since been expanded and the route extended to Gilroy.

Sadly, the gorgeous Mission Revival-style terminal at Third and Townsend in San Francisco was demolished in the mid-1970s and replaced by a more mundane facility at Fourth and Townsend, a block farther away from downtown. The station, built in 1915 for the Panama-Pacific Exposition in San Francisco celebrating the new Panama Canal—was considered one of the finest examples of Mission Revival architecture in Northern California. Today the site is occupied by an RV (recreational vehicle) park.

SP's San Francisco–San Jose suburban trains were always known simply as "commutes"; "commuter" trains were a phenomenon found farther east. A Fairbanks-Morse Train Master leads an SP commute into San Jose, California, in July 1969. Harriman-era heavyweight suburban cars such as that sandwiched by the F-M and the 1950s-era bilevels could be found in commute service into the 1980s. *Mike Schafer*

It's a hot June 22, 1990, and a brand new Cotton Belt GP60 leads a freight near Dunlay, Texas, while another freight—complete with caboose—sits "in the clear" on the siding. Freight traffic was a big blessing—and sometimes a bane—for the SP. *Dan Munson*

Chapter 4

From Beets to Berries and Staples to Stacks

Moving Freight on the Southern Pacific

Freight traffic has always been the lifeblood of Southern Pacific. Central Pacific and Southern Pacific were once the prime artery to California; towns and cities grew up along the railroad, and in its first three decades SP maintained a near monopoly on California transportation. Even as other railroads entered the California market—Santa Fe, Union Pacific, and later Western Pacific—SP was still the dominant carrier.

As competition began to encroach upon SP's all-encompassing transportation empire, the railroad fought to maintain its market share. Although railroads competed for rail traffic among themselves, and SP suffered the loss of some transcontinental traffic to the Panama Canal which opened in 1915, the most serious competition came from over-the-road trucks. By the 1920s, the infant trucking industry had begun to attack SP's traffic base, forcing the railroad to offer more-competitive service. Traditionally, railroad freight traffic moved at a glacially slow pace, and freight cars would languish in division-point yards for days. Even on the primitive highway network of the 1920s, trucks could overall move freight much faster than trains—though usually not as cheaply. As the highways improved, the competition grew more fierce. By the mid 1950s, trucks were carrying more than 50 percent of intercity freight.

AGRICULTURAL TRAFFIC

SP service was integral with California's prospering agricultural industry, and for many years agricultural products were the largest portion of SP's traffic. Pacific Fruit Express, jointly owned by SP and UP, operated thousands of refrigerator cars to haul perishables—mostly produce. Every day, PFE cars carried produce—oranges from Southern California and vegetables from the San Joaquin and Salinas valleys—by the trainload to Midwestern and Eastern markets. Southern Pacific was famous for its extensive seasonal sugar beet runs. Trainloads of wooden "racks"—special gondolas with high wooden sides—would bring the "roots" from harvest areas to processing plants around California. Sugar beets were traditionally grown in the Imperial, San Joaquin, and Salinas valleys and long trains of the wooden racks were common on both the Coast Line and Beaumont Hill. In Oregon and Northern California, timber was a staple of SP freight traffic.

BULK COMMODITIES

Solid trains of minerals and bulk commodities crossed SP's mountain grades. Oil pumped near Bakersfield would move over Tehachapi, coal from Colorado would run west over Donner, iron ore would roll west over Beaumont Hill. Copper ore would flow from mines in Arizona, and trainloads of petrol-chemicals would roll from refineries in Texas and Louisiana.

Southern Pacific trains served California ports, and considerable traffic flowed to and from these transfer points. Oakland, situated on San Francisco Bay, traditionally had been the premier West Coast port, a fact reflected in the vast scope of SP operations there, encompassing miles of yards and extensive pier facilities. However, as Los Angeles came to overshadow the Bay Area, both as a population center and as a port, SP shifted its

emphasis southward and in later years the ports of Los Angeles and Long Beach came to dominate port terminals in California.

Merchandise and boxcar traffic played a large role in SP's freight network. Although SP early on embraced intermodal traffic, the railroad remained committed to traditional carload traffic much later than other railroads. In the 1960s and 1970s SP built industrial parks at strategic locations and purchased a modern fleet of switching locomotives—one of the last large switcher fleets in the U.S.—to serve them. SP maintained comprehensive industrial trackage networks years after they had fallen out of favor elsewhere. Into the 1990s, switchers could be found lurking in back alleys in Oakland, rolling down the street in Watsonville, California, and hauling cars along tracks of the old Pacific Electric in Los Angeles.

WARTIME TRAFFIC

California had grown at unprecedented rates since John Sutter discover gold in the 1840s, but during World War II, California industry boomed as hundred of new companies settled to supply the war effort. California played a crucial roll in the war in the Pacific, hosting dozens of military installations—SP served more military bases than any other American railroad. During the war, trainload after trainload of military goods, munitions, and equipment rolled westward over the Overland Route on what the railroad coined "Tokyo Expresses." During the war, transcontinental freight traffic swelled as intercoastal shipping via the Panama Canal was curtailed. Also, the war altered traditional domestic traffic patterns. Traditionally, eastbound traffic greatly outweighed westbound traffic, but during the war this trend was reversed.

World war II was a high watermark for American freight tonnage, and Southern Pacific was the third largest freight carrier during the war. According S. Kip Farrington Jr.'s book *Railroads at War,* SP's Pacific Lines moved 37.5 billion gross ton-miles of freight in 1939, prior to U.S. involvement in the war; two years later it handled an astounding 54.4 billion gross ton-miles of freight. To help expedite the tidal wave of freight that passed over its lines during this crucial juncture, SP installed Centralized Traffic Control at critical

There was a time when seemingly endless strings of refrigerator cars were commonplace on Southern Pacific freights—and in fact many trains were comprised entirely of reefers. In this scene at Colton, California, circa 1950, Cab-Forward 4181, Class AC-8, marches through town with the first section of train 825. Its solid string of reefers is interrupted only by a diesel switcher being deadheaded. Note the brakeman on the roof of the first reefer. *R. L. Borcherding, Jim Seacrest collection*

Sugar beets were long an important agricultural traffic commodity for SP, and solid trains of sugar-beet cars were a seasonal event. Here, a fully loaded "beet rack" rolls along the Mococo Line west of Tracy, California, in May 1992. Long after most railroads ceased using wooden cars with journal boxes, SP continued to handle an ancient fleet of beet racks. *Brian Solomon*

Among the heaviest trains on Southern Pacific were the iron-ore trains running from Eagle Mountain Mine to Fontana, California, Their trip over Beaumont Hill on the Sunset Route usually required three sets of locomotives. SP SD39 No. 6925 leads a loaded ore train over the hill at Redlands, California, on April 5, 1971. *Joe McMillan*

SP's Overland Route main line via Donner Pass was once a primary route for perishable traffic rolling eastward from California. On May 27, 1970, an SP SD45 helper shoves against the rear of a perishable train near Donner Summit at Soda Springs, California. By the mid-1980s, SP had lost most of this traffic. *Joe McMillan*

choke points, especially on heavily graded single-track routes. CTC allowed the railroad to rapidly expand the capacity of its lines without massive reconstruction. The prevailing philosophy of the time was that a CTC-equipped single-track line had 75 percent the capacity of a traditional double-track line. SP's wartime CTC installations included the west slope of Tehachapi from Bena to the summit; Beaumont Hill between Colton and Indio, California; Cuesta grade north from San Luis Obispo on the Coast Line; and portions of the Shasta Route.

POSTWAR PROSPERITY

Following the war, California enjoyed unprecedented postwar prosperity, and SP's traffic remained robust. In the late 1940s SP was hauling record levels of peacetime traffic. Following the war, returning soldiers settled in California, and many new wartime businesses converted to peacetime commerce. Yet, California retained a considerable military/industrial complex as a result of Cold War hostilities. To accommodate traffic in the postwar period, Southern Pacific implemented numerous

plant improvements that enabled it to handle more traffic with greater efficiency.

In the 1950s under the leadership of the dynamic D. J. Russell—despised for his draconian passenger policies—SP focused its energy on freight business. By the 1960s SP had become an industry leader, having invested millions in its infrastructure, honing its plant into a sleek, modern freight railroad. SP experimented with new high-horsepower locomotives, expanded and centralized its yard facilities, installed hundreds of miles of CTC, lengthened sidings to allow longer trains, speeded up freight schedules, installed heavier rail, and strengthened bridges. For several years SP was operating the fastest freight trains in the U.S. When many railroads in the East faltered, SP grew and prospered—by the late 1960s it was a shining star in what had become largely an ailing industry.

SP's evolution to modern freight carrier was coincident with a reconfiguration of its route structure and traffic patterns. The dramatic growth of the Los Angeles market and the slow decline of heavy industry, port activity, and railroad shipping in the Bay Area combined with a Sunset Route preference resulted in a gradual shift away from the Overland Route and emergence of the Sunset Route as SP's premier freight corridor. Although SP's Sunset Route had taken precedence over the Overland Route as early as the 1940s, the gradual decline of the Overland route would continue for another 40 years.

DIESELS AND YARDS

Traditionally SP relied upon small- and medium-size yards situated at division points to provide freight switching. Division points, usually located near the bases of a heavy grades, often featured large locomotive-storage facilities and repair shops. Complex helper arrangements dictated train makeup, and freight trains were routinely reconfigured—mainly broken down into shorter trains—before ascending major grades. Yards at

Dunsmuir, California, Ashland and Klamath Falls, Oregon, Bakersfield and Tracy, California, and Sparks (Reno), Nevada, were just a few of SP's important steam-era facilities. SP also located yards at primary terminal areas such as West Oakland, San Francisco, Eugene (Oregon), and Los Angeles, and at key interchange points such as Ogden, Utah, Tucumcari, New Mexico, and Portland, Oregon.

The use of diesel locomotives completely changed the way SP operated freight trains, and further changes resulted with the introduction of high-horsepower locomotives. Diesels dramatically simplified mountain operations because they developed significantly greater tractive effort at much slower speeds than steam. Additionally, most SP road diesels were equipped with dynamic brakes which enabled them to haul longer, heavier freight trains than steam locomotives over SP's

Sunset at West Oakland: Southern Pacific's principal Bay Area freight yards were located at West Oakland across the bay from San Francisco, whose skyline looms distant in this 1992 scene. By the mid-1970s Oakland had lost its position as the premier West Coast port, and by the 1990s the vast West Oakland yards were just a shadow of past vitality. *Brian Solomon*

tough grades. In the Oregon Cascades, a typical steam-era train hauled by a trio of cab-ahead articulateds would weigh about 4,000 tons. After the arrival of Electro-Motive F-units on the line in the early 1950s, a typical freight weighed 6,000 tons. Later with the introduction of SD40 and SD45s, SP would routinely operate trains in excess of 7,500 tons—a nearly 50 percent increase in train tonnage in less than two decades.

The superior performance of diesels allowed SP to curtail its complex helper operations, lengthen crew districts, and scale back or close many traditional flat-switching yards. Places like Dunsmuir —a place originally known as Pusher— that had thrived as a railroad town during the steam era were quietly phased out. At Dunsmuir no longer was it necessary to reconfigure all trains climbing east on the Cascade Line to Grass Lake. Although crews still exchanged trains there and Dunsmuir served as a helper-locomotive base, most of the yard was abandoned and the roundhouse demolished. Diesels greatly diminished SP's presence in the town, and it was never the same afterward. Likewise on the upper end of the Cascade Line, Oakridge was closed as helper base and diesel helpers operated out of Eugene.

Diesels allowed for much longer trains, but longer trains required longer passing sidings and longer yards to accommodate them. In the steam era, siding lengths of 2,500 to 4,000 feet were adequate for meeting freight trains, but during the diesel era, train lengths would grow to well over 6,000 feet, and in the modern CTC era, 8,300 feet would become a standard siding length. SP upgraded its main lines, phased out small facilities, and built modern super-yards featuring "humps" (for gravity switching) and state-of-the-art diesel shops. Eugene, Roseville (Sacramento), L.A.'s Taylor Yard, and Houston's Englewood Yards became primary marshaling points and locomotive-servicing facilities.

During the 1920s Brooklyn Yard was

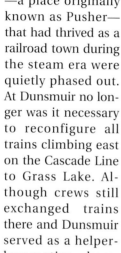

A sign at Ozol Yard depicts SP's imposing Suisun Bay Bridge on the "Cal-P" between Martinez and Benecia, Californa. The Cal-P name refers to SP predecessor California Pacific that originally ran between Sacramento and Vallejo via Davis. SP's route between Sacramento and the Bay Area has changed several times, but this line is still known as the Cal-P. Ozol Yard is situated a few miles east of Martinez and—now under Union Pacific rule—continues to serve the refineries of Martinez and vicinity. *Brian Solomon*

expanded into SP's primary facility in the Portland area. It was a significant interchange point and the assembly area for Portland-area traffic, and through the 1960s more than 2,500 cars were sorted there daily. In later years Brooklyn played a secondary role in the railroad's Oregon freight operations as Eugene became SP's primary Oregon facility. Planning for Eugene yard began in the mid 1920s, and the new facility opened in 1927. Southern Pacific greatly expanded the yard in the 1960s making it the largest railroad yard in western Oregon. Ultimately Eugene featured a hump with 32 classification tracks and served as SP's primary diesel servicing and repair facility in Oregon.

Roseville (originally known as Junction) was strategically situated a few miles east of Sacramento at the junction of the Shasta Route's East Valley Line and the Overland Route at the base of Donner Pass and had served as a primary yard since 1907. Although Theodore Judah had suggested Roseville as a major yard point in an early line profile, Central Pacific instead had built its first major yard on the west slope of Donner Pass a few miles east of Roseville at Rocklin. In the late steam era, Roseville comprised of four flat-switching yards and built trains for eastbound movement over Donner Pass and to Oregon. It reclassified traffic off the Shasta and Overland routes and directed it toward both Los Angeles and the Bay Area. Roseville was also a primary perishable-traffic hub for California and Oregon. Pacific Fruit Express maintained a comprehensive facility there which included the largest icing facility in the world. In the 1950s SP upgraded Roseville, installing a state-of-the-art computerized double hump with 49 classification tracks. The hump was arranged so that one half could be shut down during slack periods. Capable of processing more than 3,750 cars a day, Roseville had become the primary yard in Northern California.

Southern Pacific operated several yards in the Los Angeles Basin and in the 1920s built a

continued on page 79

In this two-photo sequence, a trio of "black widow" F-units lead a heavy upbound freight in the Oregon Cascades at Salt Creek while Cab-Forward 4253, a Class AC-11, works as a mid-train helper. During the steam-to-diesel transition it was not uncommon to find both types of power working together on freights in the Cascades. *Robert O. Hale, collection of M. D. McCarter, courtesy of Joe Welsh*

In the 1950s, SP modernized some its large yards with computer-controlled humps. Roseville Yard, pictured shortly after its modernization, is strategically located at the junction of the Overland and Cascade routes and played an important roll in SP's modern-day freight operations. *Robert O. Hale, collection of M. D. McCarter courtesy of Joe Welsh*

Flat-switching yards at outlying areas such as Fresno in the San Joaquin Valley supplemented SP's key hump-yard facilities. Here, three Electro-Motive units—two F-units sandwiching a passengerized GP9—are about to move out with a Bakersfield-bound train of mixed freight in the late 1960s. *Tom Taylor, collection of Ed Crist*

Continued from page 76

large new facility known as Taylor Yard that featured 500 miles of track and capacity for roughly 4,000 cars. During the late 1940s SP modernized Taylor, installing a modern hump yard designed to classify 2,900 cars daily. In addition, the Taylor complex included flat-switching yards that had a capacity for an additional 4,400 cars. The new yard complex initially allowed SP to streamline all of its L.A. yards and expedite trains out of the L.A. Basin.

Despite Taylor's enormous capacity, SP's L.A. yards were strained as traffic grew during the 1950s and 1960s, so in the late 1960s, under the direction of D. J. Russell, SP began planning an enormous new yard east of Los Angeles at Colton, California. This new facility would be built in conjunction with SP's new Palmdale Cutoff, a line which would allow freight traffic off the San Joaquin Valley Route to bypass downtown L.A. The cutoff opened in 1967 and Colton Yard opened in 1973. In the 1990s, SP phased out Taylor in favor of the newer Colton Yard, a move that contributed to massive congestion at the Colton facility.

On the Sunset Route, the focal point for freight traffic was Houston, Texas. SP lines radiated from Houston in every direction, and in the 1950s the railroad built an enormous modern yard as the primary gathering point for Sunset Route traffic originating and terminating in Texas and Louisiana. Initially Houston's new Englewood Yard featured a 48-track computerized-hump and two massive receiving yards.

The construction of modern super yards did not completely eliminate the need for all traditional facilities. Some strategic facilities survive by virtue of their location. Older facilities such as the West Oakland and El Paso terminals were expanded, and other intermediate yards such as those at Bakersfield and Sparks continued to function as marshaling points. Numerous outlying facilities such as those at Watsonville Junction and Fresno, California, and Medford, Oregon, were maintained to gather local traffic.

FAST FREIGHT

Southern Pacific's most famous freight train, the *Blue Streak Merchandise*, was rightly deemed the fastest freight train in the world on several occasions. Originally conceived by the SP subsidiary St. Louis Southwestern Railroad—prior to SP control—as a fast less-than-carload (LCL) train connecting St. Louis with Texas points, it eventually became an SP train as well. The *Blue Streak* represented Cotton Belt's attempt at winning back business lost to trucks. Under SP the train was extended all the way to Los Angeles, and ultimately it spurred a

For the Sunset Route, Houston was *the* freight traffic focal point. Southern Pacific Alco S-4 switcher No. 103 leads train No. 378 east of Cuero, Texas, on December 28, 1963. This local freight ran between Kennedy and Yoakum, Texas, on a route which more or less paralleled the Sunset Route main line. Eventually, some of the traffic gathered on the line will end up being sorted at Houston. *Joe McMillan*

The Cotton Belt freight depot at Brinkley, Arkansas, says it all. Following St. Louis Southwestern's introduction of the *Blue Streak Merchandise*, the railroad became synonymous with that train and its fast service. After SP acquired control of the Cotton Belt in the 1930s, SP capitalized on the *Blue Streak*'s reputation and expanded its service concept to SP lines. *Tom Kline*

whole family of fast trains, including the *Advance Blue Streak* and *Memphis Blue Streak*.

In the 1930s SP began running a network of fast *Overnight* merchandise trains. They were introduced in the lucrative San Francisco—Los Angeles corridor. The service proved popular and eventually SP was operating as many as 18 *Overnight* trains every 24 hours over several routes until World War II, when the *Overnight* trains had to be discontinued because of wartime traffic demands. Following the war, the railroad reintroduced fast freight service and operated named fast freights on most major routes. These trains held first-class time-card authority and—like passenger trains—operated on a strict schedule. The aforementioned *Blue Streak* trains provided service on the Sunset Route, and the Shasta and San Joaquin routes hosted several fast trains as well. The *Pacific Coast Expediter* began service between Portland and the Bay Area in 1954, and in the late 1950s SP introduced the *Starpacer* connecting Oregon and Southern California. With the success of this freight, SP added an *Advance Starpacer* in 1965. On the Coast Line, the Coast Merchandise and *Advance Coast Merchandise* whisked freight between and San Francisco and Los Angeles. The Overland Route hosted the Bay Area Extra eastbound, and *Forwarder Merchandise Special* westbound.

INTERMODAL

Although SP was not the first intermodal carrier, it played an instrumental role in the development of railroad intermodal service. Railroads had intermittently dabbled in various types of intermodal services in the years

The LAOAF (Los Angeles–Oakland Forwarder), behind a matched set of three General Electric U30Cs, climbs tortuous Cuesta grade on the Coast Line north (railroad west) of San Luis Obispo on April 6, 1980. These GE models were past their prime at this time, and it was unusual to find a solid set of them, especially on such a hot train. Ironically, the Coast Line would by the late 1980s become devoid of through freight traffic. *Brian Jennison*

On October 24, 1965, a trio of SP "Geeps" (pronounced "jeeps") lead a freight on the old San Diego & Arizona Eastern at Mananyeq, Baja California, Mexico. Southern Pacific served San Diego by way of its SD&AE subsidiary which straddled the U.S.-Mexican border. *Gordon Glattenberg*

prior to World War II. During the late 1940s, in an effort recapture business lost to the highways, several lines began trailer-on-flatcar (TOFC, commonly called "piggy back") service as second party carriers—i.e., they moved trailers of non-railroad truck lines. SP expanded upon this concept when in 1953 it initiated its own TOFC truck service using a fleet of appropriately lettered trailers that carried the railroad's own freight. SP was the first large railroad to make this bold leap into truck-train intermodal shipping. Service began between Houston and Louisiana in May and in the important San Francisco-Los Angeles market in July 1953. In 1957 SP was the single largest intermodal carrier in the U.S.

The railroad continued to innovate and in 1977 SP and railroad car manufacturer American Car & Foundry teamed up to design the pioneer "double-stack" container car—a special flatcar that could carry two intermodal containers stacked one atop the other. Two years later ACF introduced a three-unit articulated version of this equipment, then a five-unit car. SP was the first railroad to purchase double-stack equipment.

Railroad deregulation coincided with the development of advanced intermodal equipment. In 1980 the Staggers Act lifted rate restrictions that had impaired the ability of American railroads to react to changes in the

market, and this change allowed them to compete more effectively. Staggers altered the way railroads viewed intermodal shipping, and they now went after business that they had not considered before. By employing double-stacks, railroads could effectively double train capacity without increasing train length or doubling train weight. This was a great boon, particularly to a largely single-track operation like SP, and in 1981 SP inaugurated double-stack service with a dedicated SeaLand container train on the Sunset Route. Although SP pioneered double-stack operations, within a decade double-stack service was offered all around the U.S., and today stack trains are a common aspect of modern railroading.

Beginning in 1982 SP experimented with RoadRailer technology, a type of intermodal train employing truck trailers temporarily mounted on railroad wheels. Although the concept did not catch on immediately on the SP, a little more than a decade later SP would try RoadRailers again and operated a dedicated RoadRailer train between L.A. and Oregon.

TRAIN SYMBOLS

In 1974 SP implemented an alpha-numeric train symboling system. Trains were officially designated by a five-digit alpha code that was fairly straightforward and easy to understand. Every originating and terminating point was assigned a relatively logical two-letter code. The first two letters in the symbol stood for the origin point, the second two letters stood for the terminating point, and the last letter indicated the type of train. Initially some train types were indicated as follows: "F"= Forwarder, a high priority train; "T" = trailers, a piggyback/intermodal container train; "P" = perishables, a refrigerated boxcar train carrying fruits and vegetables; and "M" = manifest, a priority mixed-freight train. As a typical example of the new system, Southern Pacific's hot *Starpacer*, became known as the "LABRT"—a Los Angeles–Brooklyn Yard (Portland) trailer train. There were exceptions to the basic convention; for example SP's premier freight train, the *Blue Streak Merchandise*, was given the symbol BSMFF, which

Stack cars and TOFCs dominate freight traffic today on most major U.S. railroads, and SP was no exception. On August 18, 1991, stack train CHEGA out of Chicago—laden with both double-stack cars and more-traditional piggyback cars— threads its way through East St. Louis en route to ex-Cotton Belt trackage. *Scott Muskopf*

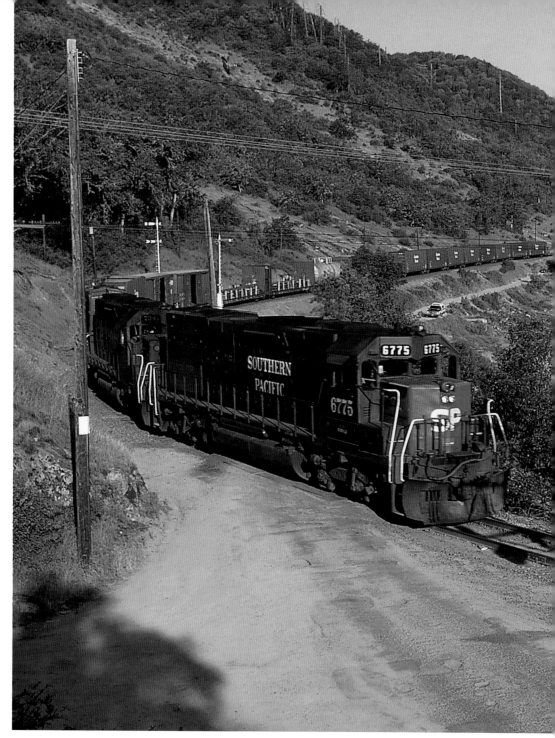

At 7:25 A.M. on May 10, 1991, the tri-weekly Eugene–Medford manifest, symboled EUMEM, rolls along the Rogue River at Ray Gold, Oregon, on SP's fabled Siskiyou Line where at the time semaphores and wig-wag crossing signals still abounded. *Brian Solomon*

stood for *Blue Streak Merchandise Freight Forwarder*. As SP's freight service evolved, the railroad made adjustments to this train-identification system.

CHANGES IN BAY AREA FREIGHT PATTERNS

Changing economic conditions combined with railroad deregulation dramatically effected traditional SP routes. Southern Pacific had gradually lost most of its once-vital produce business which greatly affected traffic moving over Donner Pass, the Coast Line, and other routes. By the late 1970s, once-busy places that had gathered produce traffic— among them Watsonville, Salinas, and Tracy— had virtually dried up. Deregulation in the late 1970s and early 1980s pushed much of the remaining business onto trucks—some of which were carried by SP competitor Santa Fe as TOFC.

The Bay Area was once SP's primary West Coast market, but a gradual loss of San Francisco and Oakland port traffic combined with the loss of heavy industry resulted in a great decline of railroad traffic from this once vital

region. San Francisco underwent the most significant changes, and by the early 1990s the Peninsula Line was nearly devoid of freight traffic. Looming over South San Francisco is a enormous hill with a large sign that proudly proclaims something that is no longer so: "South San Francisco—the Industrial City." Although the waterfront area is populated by warehouses, the occasional machine shop, and industries supporting the San Francisco airport, little actually remains of the heaviest industries. The large Bethlehem Steel mill that once stood adjacent to the tracks had been demolished, and SP's South San Francisco yard lay mostly empty. Farther up the Peninsula, cosmopolitan San Francisco, home to SP's corporate offices, was now merely a point of symbolic importance to the railroad's traffic department. Although the occasional SP switch engine still made its way into San Francisco to gather cars at Mission Bay or to make a run down along the waterfront to retrieve a load of containers, very little traffic now originated here. Most of the remaining trackage in

continued on page 88

In February 1991, near the summit of Tehachapi, a quintet of six-axle EMDs works as the mid-train helper on a BKDOL (Bakersfield to Dolores) unit oil train, the "Oil Cans." This heavy train ran daily over the Tehachapis, typically with four six-axle units on the head end of the train and five more mid-train. *Brian Solomon*

On November 2, 1980, SD9e No. 4380 leads the MJOAL (Mojave–Oakland Loaded Unit Train) out of Niles Canyon on the original Central Pacific route into the Bay Area. The MJOAL was a cement train that originated on the Creel branch outside Mojave, California. It ran over the Tehachapis and up the San Joaquin Valley to Tracy, where it turned west via Altamont Pass and Niles Canyon for delivery to Fremont, south of Oakland. SP could save a crew by running it this way rather than via Oakland. This was the last regular service on SP's Altamont Pass route, running twice a week in each direction. *Brian Jennison.*

Continued from page 85

San Francisco, including the yards at Mission Bay, lay derelict and weed-grown. SP once maintained a vast network of street trackage south of Market Street to serve industries and warehouses. By the 1990s this once-industrial area had become a fashionable district for artists and business people, and the warehouses that had once generated carload traffic instead housed popular dance clubs, photo studios, and advertising agencies.

The San Francisco waterfront was once a thriving port facility served by the San Francisco Belt Railway, a busy little shortline known for its fleet of Alco switchers. This line operated along the Embarcadero directly below the San Francisco–Oakland Bay Bridge and served a variety of wharves, warehouses, and other port-related businesses. Its tracks continued around the city, through a short tunnel, and passed the Marina to reach the Presidio army base. Although the observant tourist at Fisherman's Wharf might catch a glimpse of abandoned track in the street and the tunnel, today little remains of this railroad.

Southern Pacific once carried considerable traffic between San Francisco and L.A., but this traffic also gradually declined. By the mid-1980s SP had little need for its San Francisco yards and abandoned the vast Bayshore Yard located south of San Francisco, an enormous facility that in the 1950s had capacity for 3,788 cars and generated numerous daily trains.

SP shifted remaining Bay Area–Los Angeles business away from the Coast Line and on to San Joaquin Valley Route. In the mid-1980s SP closed the Coast Line to through freight traffic, and for several years the line hosted only Amtrak, local freight, and the occasional sugar beet train. However, the increase in both freight and passenger traffic on the San Joaquin Route prompted SP to reopen the Coast Line to through freight in the early 1990s.

OIL TRAINS

Beginning in 1983, SP began handling the largest regular unit train of crude oil. The train operated nearly daily from Bakersfield to Dolores Yard in Carson, California, south of Los Angeles. Officially the run was called BKDOL (Bakersfield–Dolores Oil) and in its later years BKDOU ("U" for unit train), but it was better known as "the Oil Can" or simply "the Cans." This train was noteworthy because of the equipment it employed and its exceptional weight. Oil was heated prior to loading and pumped into sets of continuously linked GATX Tank-Train cars. Flexible piping connections between the cars simplified loading and unloading thereby enabling a speedy train turnaround time. The Cans consisted of 11–13, six-unit tankcar sets and typically operated with about 78 loaded cars carrying nearly 2 million gallons of crude oil. The train weighed some 11,000 tons, ranking it among the heaviest regularly scheduled trains on the SP.

Typically a loaded Oil Can train would depart Bakersfield in the early afternoon and was required to meet a specific schedule dictated by the customer, Shell Oil. What made the Cans particularly interesting to railroad observers (but especially difficult for the railroad) was the tortuous move over the Tehachapis. Operating such a heavy, tightly scheduled train over such a difficult section of trackage required lots of power and careful handling. Nine high-horsepower Electro-Motive six-motor locomotives were usually assigned to this run, providing between 27,000 and 32,400 hp to lift the train over Tehachapi. Normally four locomotives would lead the train, with a five-unit manned helper set spliced in two-thirds deep in the train. Because of the tight schedule, dispatchers normally gave the Cans fairly high priority when climbing the mountain, but on occasion the train would have to take the siding on its eastward climb. Observing the long uniform black train—interrupted only by its mid-train helper—winding its way through the bucolic rolling hills of Tehachapi was a distinctly SP experience.

To reach the L.A. basin the Cans variously used the traditional route via Soledad Canyon and the Palmdale cutoff via Colton. While the Cans still roll under the Union Pacific banner, they no longer cross the Tehachapis. Shortly after the demise of the SP, a pipeline between Bakersfield and Mojave was completed that alleviated the need for the train to cross the mountains.

SATURATION ON THE SUNSET ROUTE

The phenomenal traffic growth moving east of Los Angeles on the late-era SP coupled to the railroad's inadequate physical plant contributed to severe congestion on the Sunset Route in SP's twilight years as well as during the early years of UP operation. Much of SP's capacity problems stemmed from terminal congestion, particularly in the L.A. Basin. Colton Yard, though considered by some a state-of-the-art facility in the early 1970s, was a major choke point by the early 1990s as was the El Paso terminal which had become antiquated and inadequate. Congestion at other Texas terminals compounded Sunset Route congestion. In the mid 1990s SP added some double track and lengthened sidings in a effort to ease congestion, but the situation continued to deteriorate. The situation did not improve with the advent of UP control, and in fact worsened to the point of a complete transportation breakdown.

A sad fact of railroading is that, despite its inherent efficiencies, it is very difficult to alter operations and facilities quickly to accommodate fast-changing traffic patterns. Such is the bane and blessing of rail freight transport.

On May 30, 1970, in a time-honored tradition, the conductor on an SP freight at San Jose grabs his orders. *Joe McMillan*

Southern Pacific steam still lives thanks in part to the California State Railroad Museum at Sacramento, where in 1991 two live SP locomotives pose on the museum grounds. At left, 4-6-2 No. 2472, a Class P-8, represents one of the 21 heavy Pacifics built by Baldwin Locomotive Works for SP in 1921. At right is famous GS-4 "Daylight" locomotive No. 4449—two generations and two decades removed from the 2472. *Jim Boyd*

Chapter 5

Steam Locomotives of the Southern Pacific

From Diminutive 4-4-0s to Cab Forwards and Lima Northerns

Southern Pacific and its subsidiaries relied on steam power for nearly 100 years and during that time employed some of the most distinctive American locomotives as well as some of the most common. Thousands of locomotives plied Southern Pacific rails, from the bayous of Louisiana to the mountains of California.

Early SP locomotives featured non-standard designs typical of American nineteenth century locomotive building. Harriman control of SP brought about a period of locomotive standardization between SP and his other railroads properties. There were several standard locomotive classes that used common parts permitting interchangeability. As a result a family look pervades the equipment of Harriman roads of the period.

Southern Pacific remained loyal to steam longer than most American railroads. Although many lines began to purchase fleets of diesels in the late 1930s and early 1940s, SP did not purchase many diesels until after World War II and continued to order new steam power through the war; its last new steam locomotive was delivered in 1944. Steam and diesel worked side by side for a dozen years following the war, and one of the last great steam parades in the west was the San Francisco suburban train rush. The last revenue steam on SP's standard-gauge domestic lines occurred in July 1957; the "Slim Princess" narrow gauge and lines in Mexico held on a little while longer.

Some railroads, like New York Central, scrapped nearly their entire steam fleets while others only preserved a haphazard collection of post-twentieth century switchers and light freight locomotives, but a broad cross section of SP steam power from the very first locomotives to the very last have been preserved. Southern Pacific was extraordinarily generous in donating retired locomotives to communities along its lines, and it had the foresight to preserve some of its antique locomotives built in the nineteenth century. Today some of the best examples of SP steam can be found at the California State Railroad Museum in Sacramento.

Southern Pacific's choice of fuel changed over the years. In its earliest days, SP and Central Pacific locomotives burned wood, as was common during the formative period of American railroading. By the 1870s SP was using coal, and beginning in the 1890s it began to use oil. Oil was plentiful and cheap in California, and by 1910 it was the preferred locomotive fuel. Southern Pacific was not alone in its oil use, Santa Fe and Union Pacific also had fleets of oil-burning steamers. Nonetheless, SP continued to use coal on some lines, such as the Golden State Route.

Southern Pacific had a long history of constructing its own locomotives, an unusual trait among Western railroads. Central Pacific's Sacramento Shops under the direction of Master Mechanic A. J. Stevens built a variety of locomotive types. The innovative Stevens was noted for his ingenuity and distinctive designs. He designed his own valve gear, known among railroaders as "monkey motion" because of its curious workings, he also designed feedwater heaters long before these devices were common equipment on American-built locomotives. Following Stevens' death, the railroad suspended new locomotive construction for three decades, but began building locomotives again in 1917.

Sacramento was SP's principal erecting shop, but locomotives were also built at company shops in Los Angeles, Ogden, Houston, and Algiers, Louisiana. The railroad built nearly 250 locomotives over the course of 60 years, making SP a more significant locomotive builder than many early nineteenth century locomotive companies. After 1930, all new locomotives were acquired from the three major builders—Alco, Baldwin, and Lima.

In 1913 SP implemented a alpha-numeric locomotive classification system. The system was straightforward: one or two letters determined the class followed by a number indicating the subclass. Classes were defined strictly by wheel arrangement, the letters usually representing the common type name of the wheel arrangement. Subclasses were loosely defined locomotives of the same wheel arrangement of similar specifications acquired about the same time. Subclasses were usually assigned in ascending order of acquisition, but there were

These "hogs" (C-9-class 2-8-0s built by Baldwin in 1906 and 1907) were bumped off mainline runs over Donner by the first cab-ahead Mallets 40 years before they were pictured here in 1950 at Redwood Valley, California, working as mainline helpers on the Northwestern Pacific. Within a couple of years they would be replaced for good by new Electro-Motive SD7s and GP9s. *Fred Matthews*

a number of exceptions to this general order. The basic classes are as follows:

Class	Wheel arrangement	Type
A	4-4-2	Atlantic
B	2-8-4	Berkshire
C	2-8-0	Consolidation
D	2-10-0	Decapod
E	4-4-0	Eight wheeler (American)
F	2-10-2	Santa Fe
M	2-6-0	Mogul
P	4-6-2	Pacific
S	0-6-0	Switcher
T	4-6-0	Ten-Wheeler
AC	4-8-8-2/2-8-8-4	Articulated Consolidation
AM	4-6-6-2	Articulated Mogul
GS	4-8-4	General Service or Golden State (Northern type)
MC	2-8-8-2	Mallet Consolidation
MK	2-8-2	Mikado
MM	2-6-6-2	Mallet Mogul
MT	4-8-2	Mountain
PR	2-6-2	Prairie
SE	0-8-0	Eight-wheel switcher
SP	4-10-2	Southern Pacific
TW	4-8-0	Twelve-Wheeler

EARLY STEAM

In the nineteenth century, SP's roster (including that of Central Pacific and other affiliated companies) consisted of new locomotives acquired from many different builders and a great number of engines inherited from line acquisitions. A roster of SP locomotives from the early period will reveal large numbers of Schenectady, Cooke, Rogers, and Rhode Island Works products, but a comparative dearth of Baldwin locomotives (the dominant American locomotive manufacture). This noteworthy absence is attributed to a personal feud between Collis P. Huntington and Matthias Baldwin. In the twentieth century, SP made up for its lack of Baldwin locomotives by ordering many locomotives from the prolific Philadelphia-based builder.

For about a dozen years beginning in the 1890s, SP embraced the non-articulated compound concept with considerable enthusiasm. Compounding was intended to improve engine efficiency by reusing steam exhausted from high-pressure cylinders into low-pressure cylinders before releasing steam into the atmosphere. First SP bought Schenectady-built, two-cylinder, cross-compound locomotives, a type of locomotive featuring a high-pressure cylinder on one side and a low-pressure cylinder on the other giving the engine a decidedly unbalanced appearance. After Huntington's death and the start of Harriman's control of SP, the railroad embraced Baldwin's Vauclain compound by buying them in several wheel arrangements. This four-cylinder type was designed by Samuel Vauclain and featured two sets of high- and low-pressure cylinders, one on each side of the locomotive.

Presumably Southern Pacific found that costs associated with maintaining compounds outweighed any advantages gained through improved efficiency, because by the advent of World War I most compounds had been either converted to simple (non-compound) locomotives or scrapped. Central Pacific's first locomotives were several single-drivered "bicycle" types built by the Danforth & Cooke Locomotive Works. Their small size is believed to be the result of the extraordinary demands the Civil War had on locomotive production. The most famous bicycle locomotive is CP No. 1, named for Collis Porter Huntington. This diminutive engine was used in the construction of the original Central Pacific line in the California Sierra. Later it served as a weed

The 4-4-0 American had a long life on SP and its subsidiaries. This locomotive was built by Alco's Schenectady Works in April 1914 for the Northwestern Pacific. It features several modern innovations, including piston valves and Walschaerts valve gear, but retains classic adornments from an earlier era: wood pilot, whitewall tires, and polished boiler jacketing. *C. W. Witbeck, Brian Solomon collection*

sprayer and is now preserved at the California State Railroad Museum.

The 4-4-0 "American" (sometimes called an "Eight-Wheeler") was the most common type of locomotive on Southern Pacific lines in the nineteenth century and the single most numerous type ever operated on SP. Southern Pacific and its subsidiaries variously owned nearly 700 Americans and employed them in all type of service from mainline freight to obscure branchline passenger runs. This locomotive's versatility and dependability is reflected by its exceptional longevity, despite its obsolescence. Some SP 4-4-0s operated in regular service into the 1950s.

Guy Dunscomb in his *A Century of Southern Pacific Steam Locomotives* notes that the longest-lived locomotive type and the second-most numerous was 4-6-0 Ten-Wheeler—a seemingly omnipresent locomotive found all around the system in their long productive reign. SP's Pacific Lines alone operated more than 450 Ten-Wheelers. The first 4-6-0 was acquired by Central Pacific before rails were completed over Donner Pass, and some remained active until the late 1950s. The first 4-6-0s were handsome machines resembling other motive power of the era, featuring ornamental trimmings, large diamond stacks, wooden pilots, and squared off boxy cabs.

The railroad built 21 4-6-0s at the Sacramento Shops, and these locomotives were fine examples of A. J. Stevens' handiwork, featuring his patented equipment, including his distinctive valve gear. Later 4-6-0s were more utilitarian in appearance. Southern Pacific's roster included two varieties of compound Ten-Wheelers, 18 Vauclain compounds, and 2 Schenectady cross compounds.

In later years Ten-Wheelers were often assigned to passenger runs in Oregon. They were used on everything from the *Shasta Limited* to locals on the Tillamook branch. Several 4-6-0s were assigned to the San Diego & Arizona Eastern and were used to haul trains through the spectacular Carriso Gorge between San Diego and El Centro, California.

Southern Pacific was late to embrace the 2-6-0 Mogul type, popular with many American railroads in the mid-nineteenth century. Although Central Pacific owned some of the type in 1860s, Southern Pacific Lines did not purchase large numbers of Moguls until the turn of the century—after the type had largely fallen out of favor. More than 250 Moguls served the Pacific Lines. SP had several Mogul Vauclain compounds, a very unusual compound locomotive wheel arrangement. Some SP moguls survived until the early 1950s.

Southern Pacific also owned a few 2-6-2 Prairie-type locomotives. In the 1880s seven uniquely designed 2-6-2Ts (locomotives that did not include a separate tender) were built by Sacramento Shops specifically for Central Pacific's East Bay suburban passenger services. Several of these curious locomotives later wound up in the Portland area. One was later modified and used as the Brooklyn Shop switcher where it served until the late 1930s. SP also inherited a half dozen conventional 2-6-2s with the acquisition of the El Paso & South Western in 1924.

Class A-6 Atlantic No. 3000 was rebuilt by Sacramento Shops in 1927 from an older Atlantic, making it one of the last new locomotives to use the 4-4-2 wheel arrangement. It was an atypical steam survivor in the post-World War II era. Few Atlantics lasted past the 1930s, but this one was dressed in *Daylight* colors and assigned to the Sacramento section of the *San Joaquin Daylight*. It is shown at Stockton, California in 1947. *Fred Matthews*

MASTODONS AND EL GOBERNADOR

By the early 1880s Central Pacific freight traffic moving on the transcontinental route over Donner Pass was beginning to strain the capacity of the railroad. To help ease the situation, CP's Sacramento Shops under the direction of A. J. Stevens designed a new, large, powerful locomotive that was the first to use a 4-8-0 wheel arrangement, a type known as a Twelve-Wheeler or Mastodon.

In trials on Donner the machine proved highly successful, able do the work of three or four smaller locomotives. Central Pacific, satisfied with the new machine, placed an order for 25 similar locomotives with the Cooke Locomotive Works. Central Pacific president Leland Stanford was so inspired by the new large engine his railroad had built—and always on the lookout for publicity—that he ordered Sacramento Shops to build and even larger locomotive. Practicality not withstanding, the shops followed instructions and in 1884 built a gargantuan 4-10-0—then the largest locomotive in the world—and named it *El Gobernador* in honor of Stanford.

El Gobernador was a unique machine and the only one of its wheel arrangement ever built. Its only claim to fame, however, was its great size. Stanford used the locomotive as a publicity tool, and though it served for several years as a helper locomotive in the Tehachapis, it was generally regarded as an oversized

flop. Its career was largely spent in the shop, and it was scrapped after only 10 years. The 4-8-0s enjoyed vastly more productive careers. SP owned 84 of the type, one of the largest rosters of Mastodons in the U.S., and some served the railroad for more than sixty years, making them among the longest-lived individual locomotives on Southern Pacific. Although the Mastodons were initially intended for mountain service over Donner Pass, they worked on a variety of SP's grueling grades and were common on Oregon lines.

EARLY TWENTIETH CENTURY WORKHORSES

One of the most common locomotives on the SP was the 2-8-0 Consolidation. More than 440 of these engines worked the Pacific Lines and served as SP's basic freight power for many years. The Consolidation had become a popular type on many railroads in the last quarter of the nineteenth century, but SP did not embrace the 2-8-0 in large numbers until after 1900. Initially they were assigned to mountain lines but were later used in all sorts of different freight service. SP bought a handful of 2-8-0 cross-compounds from Schenectady and some Vauclain compounds from Baldwin. Like the majority of SP's other compounds, these complex locomotives were eventually converted to simple operation.

After the turn of the century, many American railroads adopted the 2-8-2 Mikado as the

Contrast at Owenyo, California, February 1957: On the left is a standard-gauge Class MK-2 Mikado built by Baldwin in 1911; on the right on a flatcar is Carson & Colorado 3-foot-gauge 2-6-0 Mogul, No. 9 built by Baldwin in 1909 for the Nevada-California-Oregon. The No. 9 survived scraping, and today it is displayed at the Laws Railroad Museum at Bishop, California. *Fred Matthews*

95

new standard freight locomotive and nearly 10,000 Mikados were built for domestic service. Southern Pacific was slow to purchase Mikados—it did not order any until 1911, seven years after the type was introduced domestically—and operated just 83 "Mikes" on its Pacific Lines, few compared to other railroads. SP Mikados primarily served as freight locomotives, but some worked passenger trains in the Siskiyou Mountains.

For switching service Southern Pacific had a roster of more than 309 0-6-0 steam switchers on its Pacific Lines alone. These ubiquitous locomotives worked in every sort of unglamorous switching or local-type duties and are often ignored in favor of larger more distinctive models, yet they played a crucial roll in the makeup of SP trains. SP also had a small fleet of 0-8-0s, most built from parts of older locomotives at Sacramento and Houston.

"DECKS"

On many railroads 2-10-2s were known as "Santa Fes," but not on SP where Santa Fe was a dirty word often uttered with a contemptuous hiss. Southern Pacific's 2-10-2s were generally known as "Decks" short for Decapod, despite the fact that a Decapod generally refers to the 2-10-*0* type. The railroad ordered a large fleet of 2-10-2s between 1917 and 1925, the first came from Alco's Brooks Works while

Southern Pacific Class P-4 Pacific No. 2410 at San Jose, California. Southern Pacific rebuilt this 4-6-2 in 1924 from an older Class P-1 Pacific. *Fred Matthews*

On most railroads 2-10-2s were known as "Santa Fes," but not on SP where the mere mention of Santa Fe might bring scornful looks. On the SP the 2-10-2 was a "Deck," short for Decapod—never mind that Decapod usually referred to a 2-10-0. In February 1948, two F-5 Decks shove hard out of Cuesta siding on the Coast Line, pushing an eastbound freight toward the summit tunnel on Santa Margarita Hill, also known as the Cuesta grade. *Fred Matthews*

most later 2-10-2s were built by Baldwin. Most had 63-inch driving wheels, although a single locomotive was delivered with significantly smaller 57-inch drivers. Another individual locomotive was fitted with Caprotti poppet valves in 1929 in an effort of improve efficiency, but the experiment was unfavorable.

Traditionally locomotives were delivered as they were completed, typically a few at a time. However in the 1920s a large order of SP 2-10-2s had accumulated at Baldwin's Eddystone Plant. Baldwin's Samuel Vauclain, known for his sharp wit and keen eye for publicity, made the most of this situation by sending the large locomotive order west a single train. He dubbed it a "Prosperity Special" and promoted it heavily. So, what SP had originally intended as a routine locomotive order became a widely publicized event. On May 26, 1922, the Prosperity Special departed Eddystone amidst considerable fanfare. In his anecdotal book *Steaming Up*, Vauclain relates the words of Pennsylvania's U.S. Senator George W. Pepper who said "The Prosperity special will soon become prosperity general." The great locomotive train rolled westward over the Pennsylvania Railroad to St. Louis where the locomotives were interchanged to the Cotton Belt (at that time independent of SP) which brought it to Corsicana, Texas. The media quickly jumped on the story, and papers all across the U.S. were filled with photographs of the unusual "train." Along the way people came out to see the special event. It's said that SP was a little bewildered by all the pomp and circumstance and was a little late jumping on the publicity band wagon.

According to SP historian Guy Dunscomb, there were 170 2-10-2s assigned to SP's Pacific Lines. When new, the 2-10-2s were viewed as excellent heavy freight power for SP's rugged mountain lines. For a short time they began to supplant cab-ahead Mallet types in the Sierra and Oregon. Ultimately the distinct advantages of the specially designed cab-aheads prevailed in tunnel and snowshed territory, and the 2-10-2s found other niches around SP where they worked for more than three decades. Many 2-10-2s survived well into the diesel era.

For most of their careers the 2-10-2s were preferred power on the Siskiyou Line. Cab-ahead Mallets were restricted from much of rugged Siskiyou crossing, and the high-tractive effort Decks were ideally suited for this line. They were used in many types of service, working both as road and helper power on heavy freights and passenger trains alike. Heavy westbound freights leaving Ashland, Oregon, for the climb over Siskiyou Summit would often require five of the big locomotives spaced through out the train. Imagine five SP Decks at full-throttle lifting a heavy lumber-laden train through the curves below Siskiyou Summit; smoke rising high in the air, as the locomotives exert every bit of their combined tractive effort to bring the train up the better-than-3-percent grade.

Among their other assignments, the Decks were popular as helpers out of Dunsmuir, California, and Oakridge, Oregon, on the Cascade Line. As well, they were regular power in the Tehachapis and often used on the Overland Route between Sparks and Ogden.

SP and Alco designed the three-cylinder 4-10-2s for fast freight service over Donner Pass and ordered 49 of the type between 1925 and 1927. Their tenure on Donner was short lived and in later years they worked lines east of Los Angeles. The only other railroad to order 4-10-2s was Union Pacific, which also operated 4-12-2s. SP 5003 is seen in Los Angeles on Halloween 1938. *J. R. Quinn collection*

Locomotive 4008 was built by Baldwin in 1909 as a Class MC-2 and was one of the first cab-ahead Mallets. It was later rebuilt into a simple articulated and reclassified as an AC-1 and is shown as such at Sparks, Nevada, in 1947. *D. F. Richter*

THE SOUTHERN PACIFIC TYPE

Following World War I, competition from over-the-road trucking forced American railroads to speed up freight service—long drags plodding along at 10 mph or less were just not good enough any more. The need to run faster freight trains led locomotive manufactures to design a new breed of locomotives that could deliver high tractive effort at faster speeds. Alco's solution was a three-cylinder simple locomotive that featured direct piston connections with two axles—an arrangement providing greater power and more uniform torque.

In 1925 Southern Pacific and Union Pacific tested three-cylinder 4-10-2s—the greater weight resulting from the large center cylinder and its Gresley valve gear required two axles for support—and ultimately both railroads ordered the peculiar locomotive. Since this was the first application of the 4-10-2, SP denoted the new wheel arrangement the "Southern Pacific" type, while Union Pacific called its 4-10-2s "Overlands." SP's 4-10-2s were specifically designed for fast freight service over Donner Pass. Between 1925 and 1927 SP ordered 49 of these powerful locomotives— a symbolically appropriate number for a type specifically designed for operation in the California Sierra, scene of the 1849 Gold Rush. Featuring 63-inch drivers, the 4-10-2s produced 96,000 pounds of tractive effort, significantly more than SP's heavy 2-10-2s with the same-size drivers and more power than SP's early Mallets. Although the locomotives performed reasonable well on Donner Pass, there were some difficulties with their long wheel base negotiating tight curves on the mountain. Ultimately the railroad found cab-ahead simple articulateds better-suited for service over Donner Pass and transferred the 4-10-2s to the

Sunset Route for service between Los Angeles and El Paso where they survived into the mid-1950s. The last one was retired in 1955.

CAB-AHEADS

Over the years many railroads employed unique classes of steam, but no motive power fleet was as distinctive as Southern Pacific's "cab-ahead" articulateds, popularly known amongst locomotive historians as "Cab-Forwards." These big engines are a Southern Pacific trademark and well-remembered for their appearance and performance. Designed as a clever solution to a difficult problem, they came to symbolize Southern Pacific's unusually difficult operating territory.

By 1909, huge traffic volume on the Overland Route had strained the railroad's capacity, and although work had begun to double-track portions of the line, SP was also searching for a more efficient way to move trains over Donner Pass. A popular motive-power solution of the period was the double-expansion Mallet-articulated locomotive, a type of engine that debuted on the Baltimore & Ohio in 1904 and had been adapted to road service on the Great Northern in 1906.

Intrigued with the concept of powerful double engines, Southern Pacific ordered two from Baldwin in 1909. Class MC-1, they were the first 2-8-8-2s ever built, featured 57-inch drivers, and delivered 85,040 pounds of tractive effort. Like other Mallets of the period, these locomotives were delivered in the conventional format, with the cab situated behind the firebox and ahead of the tender, just the way all proper steam locomotives had been oriented since the *John Bull* of 1831. However the first trials with these engines on Donner revealed a serious problem: excessive smoke.

SP cab-ahead classes AC-4, AC-5, and AC-6 all appeared very similar. They were built by Baldwin between 1928 and 1930. The 4110 is an AC-5 built in 1929; it's leading reefer train 811 westbound in the Tehachapis near Bakersfield, California, in 1951. *Donald Duke*

The *Owl* rolls into Mojave, California, behind AC-10 4227 after surmounting the Tehachapis in July 1951. It was uncommon for cab-aheads to run in pairs. The *Owl* was SP's overnight train between Oakland and Los Angeles via the San Joaquin route, and in later years typically passed through Mojave about 7:30 A.M. It looks like it's running a little later this day. *J.R. Quinn collection*

When operating the Mallets through SP's long snowsheds and tunnels, crews found it difficult to breath and nearly impossible to see. This situation made conventional operation of Mallets on Donner impossible, so SP investigated its options, and after tests decided the best way to take advantage of Mallets on Donner was to run the engines backward. This unorthodox approach had been tried once before by SP's Bay Area narrow-gauge neighbor, the North Pacific Coast, which around the turn of the century had rebuilt a wrecked 4-4-0 in cab-ahead format. SP reversed its Mallets: the smokebox faced the tender while the firebox rode ahead of the boiler, and a specially designed cab with protective plates was installed to operate the locomotive. On a coal-burning locomotive such modifications would have been prohibitively difficult because of the great distance between the tender and the firebox resulting from the cab-ahead design, but these locomotives were oil-burners, and fuel delivery was not an issue. Initially, skeptics lambasted SP's boldness, but the cab-ahead concept worked, minimizing the smoke in the cab and vastly improving visibility. Over the next four years SP ordered 47 more cab-ahead 2-8-8-2 Mallets from Baldwin. Although cab-aheads were the rule for articulated power in snowshed territory, SP also ordered conventional Mallets for service on its Atlantic Lines.

On a snowy December 30, 1951, MT-4 Mountain 4358 pauses at Medford, Oregon, with train 329, the overnight train from Portland to Ashland via the Siskiyou Line. *Fred Matthews*

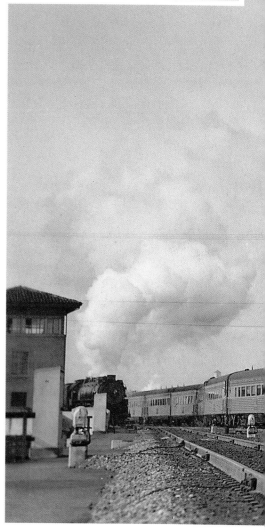

Success with the cab-ahead freight Mallets, led SP to apply the design to locomotives intended for passenger service. In 1911 it purchased 12 2-6-6-2s with 63-inch drivers, Class MM-2, for mountain passenger trains. Initially these locomotives were plagued with tracking difficulties, prompting the railroad to rebuild them with four-wheel leading trucks (making them 4-6-6-2s). Despite this modification their passenger careers were short and they ended up in freight service after just a couple of years.

By the 1920s the advantages of double-expansion Mallets had waned. Newer high-tractive-effort designs such as the 2-10-2 and 4-10-2 were giving the railroad equivalent performance without the complexity of maintaining a compound engine. Additionally the Mallets were designed for very slow speed service, and the railroad was now looking to operate faster freight trains. Southern Pacific contemplated retiring the cab-ahead concept, but instead chose to rebuild its unique articulated locomotives as simple engines. Sacramento Shops performed the conversions which entailed enlarging the boiler for greater steam capacity, casting new high pressure cylinders and equipping the locomotive with superheaters. The rebuilt articulateds were very successful; they were capable of faster mountain running and produced 10 percent more tractive effort than as compounds.

Southern Pacific was so pleased with the performance of its simple articulated locomotives it decided to purchase a fleet of new locomotives based on their design. In 1929 Baldwin delivered the first new simple-articulateds, which further improved on the performance of the older rebuilt engines. The new

Class MT-4 4-8-2 No. 4352 assists a GS-4 Northern with the westbound *San Joaquin Daylight,* storming out of Los Angeles in 1946. Two locomotives are necessary to lift train 51 over the Tehachapi Mountains and maintain schedule. The 4-8-2—a product of Sacramento Shops in the late 1920s—will be cut from the train at Tehachapi Summit. *H. L. Kelso, Ed Crist collection*

4-8-8-2s, Class AC-4, featured 63-inch drivers, used slightly larger fireboxes and cylinders, operated a higher boiler pressure (235 pounds psi versus 210 pounds psi) than the converted Mallets, and delivered 112,760 pounds of tractive effort—significantly more power than the older engines. During the next 15 years Baldwin built 8 classes of 4-8-8-2 cab-aheads for SP totaling 195 locomotives. Classes AC-4 through AC-6 were very similar to one another, and the later semi-streamlined locomotives—classes AC-7, AC-8, and AC-10 through AC-12—also shared common characteristics. The last articulateds, built during World War II, were the last new steam locomotives purchased by SP.

The cab-ahead simple locomotives were regularly used in both freight and passenger service. While the cab-ahead design was initiated for service on Donner Pass, and these locomotives defined operations there for more than a decade, they were not limited to Sierra service and roamed SP's Pacific Lines.

AC-9s

Although the vast majority of Southern Pacific's late steam-era articulateds were its distinctive cab-aheads, one group of simple articulated locomotives, the AC-9s, followed the more conventional arrangement. In 1939 SP took delivery of a dozen 2-8-8-4 articulateds from Lima Locomotive Works, Lima, Ohio. These impressive locomotives were the only Lima articulateds built for Southern Pacific and featured a semi-streamlined appearance similar to SP's Lima-built 4-8-4s. They were also distinctive because, unlike the majority of SP's Pacific Lines steam and virtually all of its other articulateds, the AC-9s were built as coal-burners. The reason for this difference

was predicated by the service for which the AC-9s were intended: as fast freight locomotives on the Golden State Route between El Paso and Tucumcari. In that territory, locally mined Dawson coal was the preferred fuel. Unlike SP's rugged mountain lines in California and Oregon, the Golden State Route was free from operating problems associated with long tunnels and snowsheds so there was no distinct advantage to the cab-ahead design.

The AC-9s were powerful, handsome machines. They featured 63.5-inch driving wheels, 24 x 32-inch cylinders, operated at 250 psi, weighed 689,900 pounds and produced 124,300 pounds of tractive effort. They were fast machines like many late-era articulateds, including Union Pacific's 4-6-6-4 Challengers and Norfolk & Western's A-class engines. The AC-9s were built for a maximum speed of 75 mph. In the days prior to strict federal regulations and with the broad open expanse of the desert between El Paso and Tucumcari, there is little doubt that some engineers let the AC-9s run their maximum speed.

Difficulties with obtaining good water in the desert, combined with the great efficiencies of diesel-electric operation, made desert routes such as SP's New Mexico lines the first candidates for total dieselization. In 1953 Southern Pacific completed the dieselization the Golden State Route. The end of steam operation also resulted in the closing of the Dawson coal fields, since the railroad had been the primary Dawson customer.

The railroad did not immediately scrap its distinctive AC-9s but instead reassigned most of them to the Modoc Line—equally open and lonely territory to the Tucumcari Line—where they worked freight for a few more years before retirement. Most of the AC-9s were

Lima built 12 conventionally oriented simple-articulateds for SP in 1939. Initially these were designed as coal-burners and assigned to the Golden State Route. Sparkling clean, AC-9 3805 pauses at Kansas City on its way to the SP. Sadly none of these handsome locomotive survived the steam era. *J. R. Quinn collection*

converted to oil operation about this time. The Modoc line was ideally suited for the AC-9s as it was free of tunnels and snowsheds, it also had been a dumping ground for aging SP steam power since its completion in the 1920s. The AC-9s would regularly haul heavy freights from Sparks, Nevada, to Fernley and then northward toward Alturas, California. The AC-9s were also favored in Modoc helper service and frequently used to assist trains from Likely to Sage Hen or from Wendel up over Viewland Hill. By 1956, the AC-9s had rolled their last miles and all of the locomotives were ultimately scrapped.

TWENTIETH CENTURY PASSENGER POWER

Atlantics

The Atlantic type was introduced in the mid-1890s specifically for fast passenger work. However the type only remained popular for about a decade and was rapidly replaced by larger, more powerful locomotives as a result of the introduction of steel passenger cars that were significantly heavier than wood cars.

In 1902 Southern Pacific bought its first 4-4-2 Atlantics, 16 Baldwin Vauclain compounds that featured unusually large drivers—at 84 inches they were the largest ever used by Southern Pacific. Later, some were rebuilt as simple locomotives with smaller (73-inch) drivers and assigned east of El Paso. SP ordered a second group of Vauclain compounds the next year. These were slightly heavier and more

powerful than the first batch and featured a distinctive appearance because they employed bulbous Vanderbuilt boilers. Although most non-articulated compounds were rebuilt as simple locomotives or scrapped by the end of World War I, some of SP's Vauclain compounds survived well into the 1920s. Later SP Atlantics were built as simple locomotives and had much longer careers than their unrebuilt compound cousins.

Southern Pacific kept ordering new Atlantics until 1911 and employed them in secondary passenger service until the early 1950s. Two Atlantics were painted in SP's colorful *Daylight* scheme for service on the *Sacramento Daylight*, the connection with the *San Joaquin Daylight* that ran between Sacramento and Lathrop, California.

Pacifics

Although Southern Pacific sampled the 4-6-2 Pacific type fairly early, it did not place large orders for Pacifics until 1911, nearly a decade after the type had been introduced. It then stayed with the Pacific, ordering them new until 1928. In 1937 SP rebuilt three Pacifics as streamlined locomotives for service on T&NO's *Sunbeam*. Another three Pacifics were draped in streamlined shrouds to resemble the Lima Northerns for service on the *Sacramento* and *San Joaquin Daylight*s.

Ultimately 112 Pacifics worked on SP's Pacific Lines; most were built by either Alco or

The Berkshire type is not commonly associated with Western railroading, however SP acquired 10 Lima-built 2-8-4s from the Boston & Maine in the mid-1940s and converted them from coal to oil operation. They ran for a short time, and were retired by 1951. Photographer Matthews caught B-1 Berkshire 3501 with a consist of refrigerated box cars south of Stockton in 1950. *Fred Matthews*

After 17 years of iron slumber in a park at Portland, Oregon, SP GS-4 *4449* was resurrected and restored to service in 1975, initially to pull the *American Freedom Train*, a transcontinental display of artifacts of American history commemorating the Bicentennial. Following those dignified duties, the locomotive was returned to its dazzling *Daylight* colors and operated on a number of excursions, including the *Louisiana World's Fair Daylight* between Portland and New Orleans. That multi-day special is shown rolling through northern California in May 1984. *Mike Schafer*

Baldwin, but two locomotives, Class P-7 built in 1917, were Lima products. Initially Pacifics were favored as mainline passenger power hauling such famous trains as the *Lark* and *Overland Limited*, but later they were bumped from such esteemed duties by more powerful locomotives, and toward the end of their careers they were largely relegated to secondary passenger duties such as commute service between San Francisco and San Jose.

In 1991, SP P-8 number 2472, one of 15 locomotives built by Baldwin in 1921, was restored to service and made a number of trips hauling excursions on SP rails.

Mountains

SP began acquiring its fleet of 83 4-8-2 Mountain types in 1923 to accommodate the railroad's heavier passenger trains. While some Mountains were built by Alco, including a few that came with SP's purchase of the El Paso & Southwestern 1924, many later Mountains were constructed at SP's Sacramento Shops between 1925 and 1930. In the 1940s many were semi-streamlined in accordance to styling predicated by the Lima-built 4-8-4s, yet

the shrouding of these locomotives was markedly more restrained and less attractive than that applied to SP's other streamlined locomotives. Following World War II, most Mountains were assigned to freight and commuter duties and as helpers.

Northerns

Southern Pacific's flashy *Daylight* 4-8-4 Northerns are among the most recognized steam locomotives in America. Perhaps only a few well-recognized locomotive types can claim greater recognition value. Southern Pacific's classification prefix "GS" for the Northern type is said to stand for "Golden State" or "General Service." The first SP Northerns were 14 Class GS-1s built by Baldwin in 1930. These conventional, unstreamlined locomotives featured 73.5-inch drivers. Initially, four were assigned to work the Texas & New Orleans, and more were transferred there in later years.

The first streamlined *Daylight* 4-8-4s were six Lima-built GS-2s designed for service on SP's colorful new *Daylight*. These were among the first new streamlined steam locomotives in

America, but unlike other lines that hired famous industrial designers to perform their styling, SP found talent within the company and the *Daylight* streamlining was the work of SP employees George McCormack and F. E. Russell Sr. The GS-2s were built to essentially the same specifications as the GS-1s, yet were intended for fast passenger service. The *Daylight* would regularly hit 80 mph, and its locomotives were capable of running at 90 mph. In 1937, Southern Pacific followed up by ordering even more impressive 4-8-4s from Lima. These *Daylight* streamliners, Class GS-3, were a little heavier, featured 80-inch drivers, and operated at 280 psi boiler pressure (compared to just 250 psi on the earlier Northerns).

The apex of the class, the definitive *Daylight* locomotive and the best known of all the SP Northerns is the GS-4. In 1941 SP received 28 GS-4s from Lima, Nos. 4430–4457. Like the GS-3s, these featured 80-inch drivers, however they were 7.5 tons heavier, operated at 300 psi boiler pressure. Externally they differed from the earlier *Daylight* locomotives by their distinctive dual-headlight arrangement including both a sealed twin-beam highlight and oscillating headlight. In 1942 SP took delivery of two GS-5s, nearly identical to the GS-4s except they weighed slightly more and were equipped with roller bearings.

In 1943 SP took delivery of its last new passenger steam locomotives, 10 GS-6s. Although these locomotives were also from Lima, their design had to adhere to strict wartime restrictions, and they were not the superlative machines of the GS-3, GS-4, and GS-5s. The GS-6s featured 73-inch drivers, weighed just 468,400 pounds, operated at only 260 psi and delivered only 64,600 pounds of tractive effort. Nor did they feature the elaborate styling of the earlier locomotives; instead of being delivered in the colorful *Daylight* paint, they were painted black. As the Cotton Belt completed dieselization, Southern Pacific inherited its 4-8-4s, which became SP's GS-7s and GS-8s.

Although SP's streamlined 4-8-4's were largely assigned passenger work, hauling the *Daylight, Coaster, Lark*, and other famous trains, they also handled freight traffic from time to time. In their later days the once-colorful *Daylight* 4-8-4s were stripped of much of their shrouding, painted black, and regularly assigned to secondary passenger runs and freights. Two of the late-era SP 4-8-4s were preserved: GS-4 4449 was displayed at Oaks Park in Portland, Oregon, while one GS-6, which hauled one of the very last steam-powered SP trains, was sent to the Museum of Transportation in St. Louis. In the 1970s, 4449 was rescued from its static state and restored to service for operation on the *American Freedom Train* which toured the U.S. in 1975–76. In 1991 it was restored to its original appearance—complete with *Daylight* livery—and has toured widely ever since. The 4449 has become an icon of not only railroading's streamlined era, but of the Southern Pacific itself.

Pickin' 'em up and layin' them down, Cotton Belt 819 does better than posted maximum speed as it crosses over highway 175 at Owentown, Arkansas, on October 17, 1993. This Cotton Belt 4-8-4 is one of several steam locomotives from SP and its affiliated lines restored to service in modern times. *Tom Kline*

SP diesels were notoriously filthy in later years, but at one time they were kept reasonably clean as illustrated by this quartet of new "black widow" SD9s rolling through Glendale, California, in 1956. Southern Pacific operated the largest roster of EMD SD9s, and some survived right to the end of the railroad in 1996. *Gordon Glattenberg*

Chapter 6

Sixty Years of Diesels on the Southern Pacific

A Fleet of Common (Yet Classic) Locomotive Models Spiced With Some Surprises

Southern Pacific had a unique relationship with the diesel locomotive. It was among the first railroads in the world to consider using diesels in road (versus switching) service and operated significant numbers of new diesel-electrics from Electro-Motive, Alco, Baldwin, Fairbanks-Morse, and General Electric, making SP one of the few large railroads to place significant orders with every major diesel builder. SP was one of only two American lines to seriously investigate freight-hauling diesel-hydraulic locomotives and owned the largest and most diverse fleet of diesel hydraulic locomotives in the U.S. Southern Pacific ordered new passenger locomotives in the late 1960s and early 1970s when few other lines considered buying new passenger power. To meet its special needs because of distinct operating conditions—notably the railroad's numerous tunnels—SP pushed the builders to design locomotives exclusively for the railroad. In the mid-1990s when most carriers were placing significant orders for new six-axle locomotives, Southern Pacific, known for its early and widespread application of six-axle diesels, continued to order larger numbers of high-horsepower four-axle locomotives for fast freight service, at that time making it the last major U.S. railroad to do so.

In 1922, SP asked Baldwin to investigate building a practical diesel locomotive—possibly the first serious inquiry by a American carrier. Little came of this investigation, and despite this pioneering interest in internal-combustion road locomotives, SP's Pacific Lines remained committed to traditional steam power longer than most other Western railroads and did not begin to seriously consider the conversion to diesel power until after the end of World War II.

The railroad had considered alternatives to steam. Long before SP contemplated replacing its steam fleet with diesels, it investigated electrifying several high-density routes. After the turn of the century, a number of American lines considered electrification as an alternative to steam power. The New York, New Haven & Hartford, Pennsylvania Railroad, and New York Central all adopted electrification early for their suburban commuter networks. NYNH&H and PRR further developed their systems into more comprehensive networks, electrifying many miles of main line and using electrification for all types of traffic, including heavy freight. Other lines such as the Virginian, Norfolk & Western, and Milwaukee Road implemented long stretches of mainline electrification. Southern Pacific considered electrifying its San Francisco–San Jose suburban service and studied electrification over Donner Pass, Tehachapi, and Beaumont Hill among other places. But other than its interurban electric lines such as those in Los Angeles, Portland, and the Bay Area, SP never embraced electrification on the same scale as other lines. Wires were never strung over the likes of Donner Pass and Tehachapi.

EARLY DIESELS

Central Railroad of New Jersey diesel-electric switcher No. 1000—considered the first commercially successful diesel-electric locomotive—had 11 years of service behind it

957   GREAT SALT LAKE CUT-OFF AT SUNSET, GREAT SALT LAKE, UTAH.

6A-H2493

SALT from Great Salt Lake Utah

The first over-the-road diesel in regular service on SP lines was the M-10004 power-car set for the *City of San Francisco,* depicted on this tinted postcard (complete with packet of salt from the Great Salt Lake) circa 1940. The M-10004 was owned by Union Pacific but operated through to Oakland via SP rails. *Mike Schafer collection*

when the first diesel operated over Southern Pacific. This pioneer movement occurred in June 1936 when Union Pacific's M-10004 articulated streamliner trainset entered 10-times-monthly service as the *City of San Francisco* between Chicago and Oakland, with SP handling the train between Ogden and Oakland. The A-B set of power cars ("A" designates a cabbed unit and "B" a cabless booster unit) for this trainset were designed by General Motors (they looked much like auto designs of the period) with carbody fabrication performed by Pullman-Standard; GM subsidiary Electro-Motive Corporation supplied the power plants. Union Pacific already had been successfully operating internal-combustion powered streamlined passenger trains for two years on its routes west of Omaha to Portland and Los Angeles.

Stretching the point a bit, the first SP-owned diesels came in 1937 with the delivery of an A-B-B set Electro-Motive E2 passenger units for upgraded *City of San Francisco* service, however SP initially owned this locomotive set jointly with Union Pacific and Chicago & North Western. When they were new these beautifully streamlined locomotives—distinctive with their inward-sloping noses and side portholes—carried a 5,400-hp rating, making them the most powerful diesel passenger locomotives in the world at that time. Like UP's other *City* streamliners, the locomotives and cars were painted in UP's Armour yellow and autumn brown, although the logos of all three operating roads appeared on nose of the E2 A-unit. Upon the termination of joint ownership of the three-unit set in 1948, the A-unit became entirely owned by SP, was repainted in red-and-orange "Daylight" colors, and acquired the nickname "Queen Mary."

Despite the popularity and success of the diesels on the *City of San Francisco,* SP was reluctant to buy road diesels entirely of its own until after World War II, although its Cotton Belt affiliate acquired a fleet of 20 Electro-Motive FTs—the first mass-produced road-freight locomotive. In this conservative approach, Southern Pacific differed from its competition. While SP cautiously eyed the diesel, Santa Fe purchased a vast fleet of Electro-Motive FTs.

In the late 1930s and early 1940s, SP began purchasing new diesel switchers, first from Electro-Motive and later from Alco and Baldwin. The first assignment of the first Electro-Motive switchers was SP's West Oakland yards on April Fool's Day 1939.

Early on, Southern Pacific rostered its Pacific Lines diesels separately from those used on its Texas & New Orleans subsidiary and Cotton Belt affiliate. T&NO locomotives were numbered lower than 1000 while SP diesels held four-digit numbers. Cotton Belt locomotives, though painted in SP family colors, were lettered for Cotton Belt—a practice that continued nearly to the end of the SP itself.

SOUTHERN PACIFIC GOES ALL-DIESEL

World War II placed an extraordinary strain upon all American railroads, and following the war most were in desperate need of new locomotives. Southern Pacific was no exception.

Although SP had remained loyal to steam before the war, by 1945 it was clear that diesels were a more efficient way to move trains. Further, the railroad was now managed by more progressive people, including D. J. Russell, who recognized the great advantage of diesel operations. Within five years of the introduction on its first road diesels, SP had purchased more than 1,000 diesel locomotives. Yet it would take more than a decade for SP to completely dieselize its operations. While SP tested the locomotive market, Electro-Motive diesels would play the largest and most important role in its new motive-power fleet.

Diesels required special maintenance facilities, and one of the heavy initial costs of dieselization was the construction of diesel shops and maintenance areas. In the early years, SP set up diesel shops in Los Angeles and Roseville, California, Ogden, Utah, and San Antonio and Houston, Texas. As diesel operation became more prevalent, the railroad built numerous additional facilities at strategic locations. One of the great advantages of the diesel was that it required far less service and maintenance than steam locomotives, so although there was a high initial capital investment of building specialized facilities, the railroad ultimately saved a fortune by closing many steam-era shops made redundant and unnecessary by diesel operation.

Day or night, Southern Pacific diesels were immediately recognizable by of their extensive use of lights. Where some lines were content with just a headlight, SP locomotives were equipped with headlights, oscillating headlights—often called Mars lights, after one manufacturer of such equipment (and later, candy bars), red oscillating lights, and class lamps. Later diesels featured the distinctive combination of dual sealed-beam headlights, dual white oscillating headlights (usually made by Gyralite), and a single red oscillating headlight. No other railroad in the nation boasted such a prolific use of locomotive headlamps. This extensive practice was curtailed following the ill-fated Santa Fe/SP merger proposal and afterward, SP headlight installations conformed more closely to the national norm. Mars lights and class lamps were removed, and most locomotives were equipped with track-level "ditch lights" and rotating roof-top flashing lights like those used on tow trucks and highway equipment.

ELECTRO-MOTIVE FIRST GENERATION

After the war, SP continued to rehabilitate its passenger-train fleet—a program initiated during the Great Depression—and introduced a host of new streamlined passenger trains, but unlike their pre-war counterparts, these new trains featured diesels instead of steam as power. SP's first road diesels were a small fleet of EMD E7s bought in 1946 and 1947 and painted in a vermilion and silver scheme to match the *Golden State Limited*. Initially the E7s primarily worked east of Los Angeles. A few months after the E7s, SP's first road freight diesels from EMD, a small fleet of F3s, arrived. Initially these were also assigned to the Sunset

SP's first wholly owned road diesels were 15 E7s (10 A-units, 5 B-units) intended for service on the Sunset Route (E-units performed best in flatland duties). They were delivered in an austere scheme of silver and vermilion. *Andover Junction Publications archives*

Route, but a short while later they also began working in the Tehachapi Mountains. The success of the F3s led SP to purchase a large fleet of EMD carbody cabs and boosters, first F3s and then F7s and even some FP7s which could be used for either passenger or freight service. All were delivered in a striking black, silver, and orange paint scheme—now known universally as the "black widow" scheme—and the four-axle EMD cabs became commonly known simply as "Black Widows."

The F-unit ushered in a new era in SP motive power. The earlier era was dominated by SP's distinctive Cab-Forward or "cab ahead" steam locomotives and this one by EMD's trademark "bulldog nose." The Black Widows worked all over SP's vast system. A large number of Black Widow F-units were based at Roseville and shortly after their arrival rapidly displaced cab-ahead articulated locomotives on mountain freight. By the late 1940s

the sounds of EMD's 567 engine were shaking the rocks at Yuba Pass, reverberating in the sheds above Donner Lake, and echoing through the Sacramento River Canyon, replacing the long familiar sounds of articulated steam locomotives with their distinctive syncopation. Although some cab-aheads dated back more than 30 years, others were quite new. Putting the locomotive's respective ages in perspective, the oldest Black Widow F-units were only three years younger than the newest cab-ahead articulated. The Fs did not replace steam in the Cascade Mountains until the early 1950s, nearly five years later than on the Sunset Route. Initially four unit sets of Fs were used in Eugene (Oregon) helper service, eliminating the need for mid-train cab ahead articulateds to be cut in at Oakridge. This made for a transitional motive power arrangement featuring steam on the point of westbound freights (those traveling uphill from Eugene

SP began dieselizing its freight operations with Electro-Motive F-units, initially F3s and later F7s. Southern Pacific F7A No. 6284, resplendent in "Black Widow" livery, rolls past a steam-era coaling tower at Lordsburg, New Mexico, on February 4, 1962. Coaling towers were rare on SP because after 1900 most of its steam power burned oil. *Gordon Glattenberg*

toward Cascade Summit) and diesel mid-train.

Ultimately SP amassed a fleet of more than 700 EMD F-units, making the Black Widow F-unit one of the most common faces on the railroad. For a decade, steam and diesels co-existed on SP. Although steam survived in pockets until 1957, after 1955 there was little steam left on SP's mountain main lines, and diesels—largely EMDs—were doing most of the work. Yet, the F-unit had a comparatively short life on SP, and nearly as quickly as they

came they vanished. After only two decades of service, SP's F-units were already candidates for trade-in and retirement. Unlike switchers and road-switchers, F units were most useful as mainline locomotives. Their attractive streamlined carbody design had proved limit-ing in actual service—they were cumbersome in switching duties and more difficult to main-tain in routine servicing because they did not have engine side doors as on "hood" or road-switcher units. As significantly more powerful

An exceptionally clean FP7 clad in the latter-day "tomato nose" scheme leads a passenger Extra at Sacramento, California. SP maintained a small fleet of passenger Fs in addition to its large fleet of freight Fs. The FP7s worked well in mountain territory such as over Donner Pass on the Overland Route. *Herb Johnson.*

SP's "Cadillacs"—the SD9s—were long-lived and widely dispersed, though they were particularly plentiful on Oregon lines. Three of the six-axle hood units charge across the Yaquina River near Pioneer, Oregon, on the Toledo branch in August 1979. *Brian Jennison*

Freshly painted GP9 No. 3190 together with a later GP20 model and another GP9 lead a westbound Coast Line freight at San Jose in August 1977. In the distance, another GP9 has a San Francisco-bound commute in tow. The air tanks atop the 3190 indicate this to be a passenger "Geep" that has found weekend freight duty. *Herb Johnson*

locomotives became available, the usefulness of the F-unit fleet waned. In the mid-1960s SP began trading in its Fs, many still wearing the same black-widow paint in which they were delivered, although badly faded and worn after years of demanding service. Many freight Fs ran out their final days in Oregon, working local assignments on branches. By the early 1970s, most of SP's Fs were gone, save for the fleet of passenger units that survived well into the Amtrak era that began in 1971. Clean, sparkling EMD FP7s in SP's handsome scarlet and gray paint regularly hauled Amtrak's *Reno Fun Train* over Donner Pass long after the other Fs had vanished from the scene.

Southern Pacific later augmented its E7 fleet with a single E8 and a small fleet of E9s that were equipped with dynamic brakes—an uncommon accessory for E-units. The Es regularly hauled LA-based passenger runs and were common power on the Sunset Route and Coast Line.

In the early 1950s, Electro-Motive—a division of General Motors since 1941—followed the lead of its diesel competitors by introducing a six-motor road-switcher. Southern Pacific, which sampled six-motor units from Baldwin, Alco, and Fairbanks-Morse, embraced the EMD six-motor road-switcher before any other American line. Electro-Motive initially felt that six-motor road

switchers were highly specialized locomotives and gave them the model initials "SD" for "Special Duty" while four axle-road-switchers were given the initials "GP" for "General Purpose." Southern Pacific ordered the first SD7s, which carried enormous "ashcan" Mars lights which seemed out of proportion with the rest of the locomotive. Later SP bought a significant fleet of SD9s (see lead photo for this chapter), more than twice as many as any other road in America. Some SD7s worked SP subsidiary Northwestern Pacific in their early years, and later many were rebuilt for yard work. They survived at Roseville well into the 1990s, giving them more than four decades of service on the railroad. The SD9s were delivered in the same black-widow paint as SP's EMD F-units, but came to be known by railroaders and observers simply as "Cadillacs"—presumably for their solid ride quality. Later they were painted in scarlet and gray, the scheme for which they are probably best remembered. A few also received the short-lived Southern Pacific–Santa Fe "Kodachrome" merger scheme—yellow, red, and black—which they carried for nearly a decade after ICC's rejection of the SPSF merger. The nickname referred to the familiar colors of a box of Kodachrome film. Southern Pacific's SD9s were solid reliable locomotives that enjoyed unusually long productive, careers on the railroad—some lasting nearly to the very end of the railroad itself as an independent corporate entity—while working a great variety of assignments. So common and versatile, the SD9 at times must have seemed omnipresent on SP's Pacific Lines. Early on, the 1,750-hp SD9s served as the diesel equivalent of SP's 2-10-2 ersatz "Decapods." Like the "Decks," the SD9s were multi-axle, high-tractive-effort locomotives that worked short grade-intensive districts such as Tehachapi and the Siskiyou lines. Later, as more powerful six-axle locomotives were purchased, the SD9s were assigned other duties. The Cadillacs were the preferred Oregon branchline power, and they continued to work the Siskiyou Line, although rarely on the head-end of road freights. In the 1970s SD9s were typically used as helpers over Siskiyou Summit, and into the 1990s they regularly hauled local freights, typically in pairs. They worked SP's other long Oregon branches, the Toledo, Tillamook, and Coos Bay lines, where it was common to find as many as six SD9s in tandem on a heavy train. The SD9s were regularly assigned as helpers on Cuesta grade on the Coast Line, in the Cascades and Tehachapis, and occasionally over Donner Pass. As late as the early 1990s, the SD9s were regularly assigned to local work in the Bay Area, out of Roseville, and on the Northwestern Pacific "Sprint Train"—the freight that in later years ran from Willits to Napa Junction and Fairfield in Northern California. Two SD9s were equipped for passenger service, but after a stint on the San Francisco–San Jose commutes, were usually assigned to freight trains.

Although Southern Pacific did not own GP7s—EMD's first popular road-switcher type, the four-axle counterpart of the SD7—the railroad bought hundreds of EMD GP9s between 1957 and 1959. Like the SD9s, the GP9s were delivered in black widow paint. They served the railroad for roughly 35 years, working numerous different jobs. They held down local assignments all across Texas and Louisiana, in California's Central and Salinas valleys, and in Oregon's fertile Willamette Valley. Some GP9s were equipped for passenger service and worked Bay Area commutes until the arrival of CalTrain F40PHs in June 1985. In later years GP9s were largely used on branchline and local freights, although occasionally the odd GP would find its way into a road set.

Beginning in the late 1960s, SP decided to maintain its investment in its solid, reliable, and well-proven EMD road-switchers by rebuilding the locomotives at its Houston and Sacramento shops. Nearly the entire fleet of locomotives underwent rebuilding, a project that significantly lengthened their active life span. Although these EMD road-switchers were less than ten years older than the F-units—locomotives with which they shared many important similarities, including

PA 6041 has been teamed with Electro-Motive E-units on train 99, the *Coast Daylight*, standing at Los Angeles Union Passenger Terminal in the late 1950s. SP's Alco PAs tended to be assigned to mountain territory such as the Shasta Route and Overland Route. Their last haunt, in fact, was on the Overland Route working the *City of San Francisco* between Oakland and Ogden. *Alvin Schultze*

Alco RS32s Nos. 4000 and 4001 stand side by side at Bayshore Yard in San Francisco in 1975. SP had but a modest fleet of Alco's RS-series locomotives. *Brian Jennison*

One of SP's Alco Century 643H hydraulics has the uncommon assignment of assisting a passenger train—possibly a special move—at the 16th Street Station, Oakland, date unknown. *Ed Crist collection*

important components such as the 567 prime-mover—the road-switchers lasted more than twice as long as their carbody counterparts and significantly longer than road-switchers built by Alco, Baldwin, and Fairbanks-Morse.

AMERICAN LOCOMOTIVE COMPANY

In 1939 Southern Pacific bought three Alco HH660s (660-hp high-hood) switchers, the first members of what would become the railroad's comparatively large Alco fleet. Southern Pacific continued to purchase Alco switchers into the mid-1960s and ultimately ordered nearly 300 of them. Although Alco's S1 through S4 switcher series were relatively common, very few railroads ordered Alco's S6 switcher, and with 70 of that type, SP had by far the largest roster of them. SP was also one of only

a handful of railroads to purchase Alco's C415 center cab switcher introduced as part of Alco's Century line in the mid 1960s.

Electro-Motive had the jump on the passenger diesel market, having introduced its first E-units in the mid 1930s, and most American railroads preferred EMD diesels for their passenger trains. Electro-Motive's E7 was the most popular passenger model and more than 500 of them were sold nationwide. Although SP operated a fleet of E-units, it bucked the national trend by placing large orders with Alco for its PA (cab carbody) and PB (booster) passenger units. The PA used Alco's model 244 V-16 engine; the PA/PB1s developed 2,000 hp while PA/PB2s developed 2,250 hp. The first PAs arrived in May 1948, and ultimately SP wielded the largest roster of PA/PBs owning 66

units—including two owned by Cotton Belt. Southern Pacific was also among the last railroads to operate them, maintaining its fleet until 1967. The PA's distinctive look, with a handsome streamlined design featuring an impressive six-foot long nose looked great in SP's flashy Daylight scheme, and certainly a trio of these impressive locomotives leading the *Shasta Daylight* was one of the visual highlights of the streamlined era.

Like most of Southern Pacific's diesels, the PAs were equipped with dynamic brakes. For this reason and their pulling power, PA's were the preferred passenger locomotive on heavy mountain runs and were regularly assigned to Overland and Shasta Route trains. A number of PAs were equipped with snowplows to cope with heavy mountains snow. Yet, PAs were not excluded from other routes. Early on, about a half-dozen PAs worked out of Los Angeles on the Sunset Route. The Coast Line's *Lark* would regularly use PAs in that train's later years, and PAs were frequently used on the *San Joaquin Daylight* on the inland route. A dozen PAs worked T&NO lines and regularly handled assignments on the Sunset Route, as well as on the Dallas-Houston *Sunbeam* and *Hustler* runs. Initially the Alcos were used in matched sets of three in an A-B-A configuration, but in later years sets of four or more PA cabs were quite common. Toward the end of the passenger era, a solitary PA might be assigned to one of SP's lesser passenger trains, sometimes with just one or two cars. Southern Pacific adopted its standard scarlet-and-gray paint scheme in 1959 and discontinued the more complex Daylight livery. By the early 1960s many PAs had been painted into this modern scheme.

Southern Pacific had a moderate fleet of Alco road-switchers comprised of various four- and six-axle models. Cotton Belt had 17 RS3s built in 1951 and 1952 while SP's Pacific Lines rostered RS11s, RS32s, RSD5s, RSD12s and RSD15s.

In the mid-1960s, SP bought a fleet of six-axle Alco Century locomotives. In 1964 it bought three Century 643Hs—discussed in greater detail later in this chapter—and 29 conventional C628s over the next year; 15 Alco C630s followed a year later. Initially SP assigned its conventional six-axle Centurys to work the steeply-graded mountain territory east of Roseville. They hauled trains over Donner Pass and up past Mt. Shasta, however the six-motor Centurys did not perform satisfactorily in mountain service and were quickly

withdrawn and assigned less taxing duties elsewhere on the railroad, leaving the hard mountain work to SP's growing fleet of six-axle EMDs. Although Century-series locomotives are held in high regard by observers for their superior aesthetic attributes, when it came to performance SP felt they were inferior. The C630s suffered from numerous mechanical flaws and SP management was especially dissatisfied with their performance. These were the last new Alco locomotives purchased by SP, and only a few years after their delivery Alco exited the new locomotive market. By 1973 the big Centurys were largely relegated to yard and transfer duties in Los Angeles and New Orleans.

Southern Pacific retired the last of its Alcos in the early 1980s, along with a large portion of its older, non-EMD locomotives. The railroad had just purchased large numbers of new locomotives and their delivery unfortunately coincided with a nationwide economic recession that left SP with less traffic and lots of locomotives. Unusual models with special parts requirements or shop-intensive antiques were quickly dropped from active service, a trend that prevailed across the country.

BALDWIN LOCOMOTIVE WORKS

Southern Pacific purchased two 660-hp Baldwin VO660 switchers in 1941, and later bought 25 1,000-hp VO1000 switchers. The railroad remained loyal to the traditional steam locomotive builder for a decade into the diesel era and assembled a roster of 192 Baldwin diesels—among the largest such fleets in the U.S. Through the 1940s SP continued to acquire four-axle Baldwin switchers and operated ten DS4-4-1000s, and 59 S12s. These

Southern Pacific's Baldwins were delivered in a black-and-orange livery as illustrated on restored AS616 No. 5208 at Sacramento in 1991. Though builder Baldwin was a titan when it came to steam-locomotive production, its diesels were not widely embraced, although SP rostered a sizeable fleet. *Herb Johnson*

newer locomotives employed a turbocharged six-cylinder prime mover instead of the older naturally aspirated eight-cylinder VO engine used in earlier models. Baldwin believed the turbocharged engine was more reliable and more fuel-efficient. Initially some Baldwin switchers were assigned to yards in the Bay Area, but in later years they were primarily used in the Los Angeles Basin. Many Baldwin VO switchers were transferred to SP's interurban affiliate, Pacific Electric, and lettered accordingly.

In the late 1940s, Baldwin's DR4-4-15 "sharknose" demonstrators toured the SP and made a noteworthy showing on the railroad's difficult Siskiyou Line. Although SP never purchased any Baldwin cab units (very few railroads did), it did order a large fleet of Baldwin's six-axle road-switchers and sampled Baldwin's A-1-A (six-axle trucks with a non-powered center axle) DRS6-4-15 type. When Baldwin introduced the six-axle, six-motor AS616 road-switcher, SP was quick to see the value of this type of loco-motive. Six powered axles gave a locomotive significantly better adhesion, making them well-suited to SP's grade-intensive profile. The first six-axle Baldwins arrived in 1948. SP tried the locomotives in various types of service all around the railroad but found them best suited as helper locomotives. A number of AS616s were assigned as helpers on the Siskiyou Line where they worked mostly out of Ashland, Oregon. The railroad also had several unusual "cow-and-calf" six-axle sets (the "calf" being a cabless road-switcher permanently assigned with a cabbed locomotive). These curious locomotive combinations were normally assigned to hump-yard duties at Eugene, Oregon, and at Englewood Yard in Houston, Texas. Toward the end of their careers, the Baldwin road-switchers were concentrated around Eugene yard. Some were later sold to lines in Mexico.

FAIRBANKS-MORSE

Fairbanks-Morse, known for its distinctive opposed-piston prime movers, entered the diesel-electric locomotive market relatively late and exited fairly early. Yet, during the decade it produced locomotives F-M induced many carriers to try its products and sold a fair number of locomotives. Southern Pacific purchased only 61 F-M locomotives, but was one of the more enthusiastic operators of these locomotives and maintained its fleet into the early 1970s, long after most major carriers had retired their F-M fleets. However, in the grand scheme of SP's comprehensive dieselization, its F-M roster is just a footnote.

The railroad bought its first F-Ms in 1952— some five years before it purged steam from its Pacific Lines—and bought its last F-Ms only a few years later. These early F-Ms were

six H12-44 switchers, followed a year later by ten more of the same type and another nine in 1955. They primarily worked Bayshore Yard in San Francisco.

The railroad's most prominent and best remembered F-Ms were its small fleet of 16 H24-66 Train Master locomotives billed as the world's most powerful road-switcher when they were new in 1953. Each six-axle locomotive generated an astounding 2,400 hp, making them significantly more powerful than Electro-Motive's comparable 1,750-hp SD9. The railroad was pleased with F-M's demonstrators and purchased two of them, followed by an additional 14 locomotives. Initially the big six-axle Train Masters worked in heavy freight and passenger service in Texas and New Mexico, but by the late 1950s SP sent them to San Francisco to work the Peninsula commute

trains—probably because of the Train Master's ability to quickly accelerate under load—and they remained in this service for the next two decades. On weekends, when the powerful locomotives were not needed for passenger work, SP employed them in area freight service. It was the only fleet of F-M Train Masters operated by a Western railroad.

THE SECOND-GENERATION DIESEL ERA OF SP

The last steam had only been retired for a few years when SP began looking at the next generation of diesel locomotives. Diesels had allowed the railroad to run longer, heavier trains with fewer crews and few engine changes than with steam locomotives. The effect of the diesel on SP operations was profound. Yet, SP was still looking for additional ways to improve operations. By the early 1960s

ESPEE'S HYDRAULIC DIESELS

In the early 1960s Electro-Motive Division ruled the new locomotive market. Steam had been successfully purged from American main lines, and, save for Alco, there was little competition for new locomotive orders. Although a large supporter of EMD products, SP not entirely satisfied with the size of locomotives offered by Electro-Motive. Wanting more powerful locomotives, SP looked to Germany for a solution. The German manufacturer Krauss-Maffei had perfected the diesel-hydraulic locomotive which potentially offered greater horsepower and more tractive effort than domestic diesel-electrics. In 1961 Southern Pacific and Rio Grande each imported three carbody-style Krauss-Maffei locomotives, which employed two Maybach V-16 diesel engines and a Voith hydraulic transmission system (used in lieu of electric traction motors). K-M rated the locomotives at 4,000 hp. While Rio Grande was dissatisfied with the locomotives, SP placed a repeat order with K-M in 1963 for an additional 15 locomotives. These were built as road-switchers, but also used the Maybach engines and Voith transmissions. They were designed to work either in multi-

ple with each other or with diesel electrics. In 1964 SP acquired Rio Grande's three K-Ms which worked SP lines in Rio Grande's characteristic gold and silver paint with SP lettering. SP remained interested in the potential of diesel-hydraulic power and that year ordered three Alco C-643Hs, the most powerful hydraulic locomotives to join its roster. The C-643Hs used two Alco 251 prime-movers and the Voith transmission, and generated 4,300 hp.

All the hydraulics were based at Roseville. Initially they worked the Sierra and Oregon mountain lines, but following difficulties in this service, they were usually assigned more level territory in the San Joaquin Valley. One of the flaws with the hydraulics was their unusually high maintenance requirements which placed them at a distinct disadvantage in comparison with diesel-electrics. SP ultimately rostered 21 diesel-hydraulic locomotives, the largest roster in the United States. Although diesel-hydraulics are still popular in Europe and Japan, Southern Pacific had found more cost effective ways to fulfill its motive power needs and all of its hydraulics were out-of-service by 1970.

Southern Pacific and Denver & Rio Grande Western both imported German-built Krauss-Maffei diesel-hydraulic locomotives. D&RGW gave up on the experiment early and conveyed its three K-M cabs to SP. One of the former Rio Grande locomotives leads a perishable train near McFarland, California, on the San Joaquin Valley Line on August 15, 1964. By 1970, SP also had given up on the diesel-hydraulic concept. *Gordon Glattenberg*

its was not uncommon to find 10 or more F-units hauling trains over SP's mountain grades. SP wanted to run longer, heavier trains with fewer locomotives. To this end, SP embarked on an experimental path in regards to locomotive development and acquisition.

In the early 1960s Southern Pacific sampled EMD's turbocharged GP20. This locomotive used the same basic 567 prime mover as the earlier GP9 but extracted 2,000 hp from it by using a turbocharger—a technology that signaled the start of the "second-generation" diesel era, since first-generation diesels were nearing the end of their service lives and railroads were seeking replacements. In 1963 SP and Cotton Belt picked up 18 EMD GP30s, and beginning in 1965 they acquired 182 GP35s, primarily for fast freight service on the Sunset Route. In addition, SP also ordered three DD35Bs—monster eight-axle cabless locomotives that were really little more than two GP35s riding a common underframe; they were intended to operate between two GP35s. Typically the DD35s worked east of L.A.

High-horsepower four-axle locomotives such as the GP35 were ideally suited for a high-speed freight application. At approximately the same time SP acquired the GP35s, it was also acquiring large numbers of General Electric U25Bs discussed in greater detail later. After this initial binge for high-horsepower four-axle locomotives, SP became intrigued with the advantages of six-motor power, and although SP bought some GP40s for Cotton Belt in 1966 and three GP40Ps for passenger service in 1974, during the next decade it concentrated on building its six-motor fleet.

In the 1960s and 1970s SP found no locomotive design better suited to its grueling mountain grades than EMD's high-horsepower six-axle locomotives. Two decades after F-units had taken over mountain mainline runs from cab-ahead articulateds, EMD's modern high-horsepower SDs replaced the F-units. In the mid 1960s, EMD introduced its 645 engine, a significantly more powerful prime-mover than its earlier 567 engine that had been the mainstay of its locomotive pro-

SP's interesting diesel roster is aptly portrayed in this 1965 scene of an eclectic assortment of power led by GP35 7412 rolling through El Paso. There are both first- and second-generation diesels in this riot of motive power, including one of SP's three eight-axle GE U50s. *Gordon Glattenberg*

duction for more than 20 years. With this new
engine, EMD introduced a line of new, powerful SD-series six-motor locomotives.

Although SP purchased a small fleet of
2,500-hp SD35s in 1965 (a locomotive that featured the 567 engine), the two most popular
six-motor models on SP would be variations of
the 3,000-hp SD40, which employed the 16-
cylinder 645E3 engine, and variations of the
3,600-hp SD45, which used the 20-cylinder
645E3 engine. In 1964, Electro-Motive's SD40X
demonstrators toured the SP, and clearly the
railroad was impressed with the model. In
1966 SP acquired 79 SD40s and its first SD45s.
Southern Pacific embraced the 20-cylinder
SD45—a trend which again differed from most
other U.S. railroads which used EMD's six-
motor locomotives. Southern Pacific bought
more than 600 of the roughly 1,700 20-cylin-
der locomotives sold by Electro-Motive,
including 357 SD45s (including those purchased for Cotton Belt)—more than twice as
many SD45s than any other railroad. In later
years, when many other lines had retired their
20-cylinder locomotives, SP continued to

operate SD45s and chose to rebuild them
(continuing with 20-cylinder power plants,
which some railroads felt were high maintenance) rather than to trade them in. By the
mid-1990s, SP's 20-cylinder fleet was not only
still the largest but among the very last. Even
after Union Pacific assumed control of SP in
September 1996, the reverberations of SP's 20-
cylinder monsters, noted for their exceptionally low powerful rumble, still echoed along the
Western canyons which they first invaded 30
years earlier.

Generally Southern Pacific was very pleased
with the performance of its SD40s and SD45s,
however, when EMD was testing its 4,200-hp
SD45X demonstrators on the railroad in
1970–71, SP noted that the locomotives did not
give optimum performance when climbing
through snowshed and tunnel territory in the
Sierra and Cascades. This presented a significant operating problem for the railroad, one
comparable to its difficulties with the early
Mallets: SP wanted to assign its most powerful locomotives to its most demanding territory and needed to find a way of obtaining

Trailed by two Tunnel
Motor SDs, SP SD45
No. 9049 pops out of
Tunnel 3 at Cascade
Summit in Oregon on
January 31, 1981. SP
was a big proponent of
the 20-cylinder
locomotive. Later models
were redesigned for
maximum performance
in tunnels and
snowsheds. The SD45
has the "full house" SP
light package, complete
with oscillating Mars
light and red emergency
light. The SP's light
package was distinctive
and gave its locomotives
character while
providing extraordinary
grade-crossing
protection for the
unwary motorist. *Brian
Jennison*

maximum power when operating through the mountains. The problem with the Mallets was that exhaust gases in the tunnels and sheds seriously affected crews; the problem with the EMD six-motors also occurred in tunnels and snowsheds, but it affected locomotive performance rather than crew health. On the SD45X, air intake vents were located at the top rear of the locomotives. When the units were working at full throttle in tunnels and snowsheds they had a tendency to also exhaust the available air supply which caused engine overheating and degraded locomotive performance. SP and EMD engineers worked together on this problem and came up with a unique solution by redesigning the locomotive air-flow pattern; intake vents were relocated from the top of the locomotive to the level of the running boards. Southern Pacific took delivery of specially designed six-motor EMDs in both 16-cylinder and 20-cylinder models—locomotives which like the cab-ahead Mallets were specially designed for operation in California's Sierra Range. These locomotives had a "T" (for "Tunnel") in their model designation and have been popularly known to observers as "Tunnel Motors." The 3,600-hp SD45T–2 was a variation of the SD45; it was 70 feet 8 inches long and featured the 20-cylinder engine while the SD40T–2 was a variation of the SD40 and likewise generated 3,000 hp using the 16-cylinder 645 engine. The first SD45T–2s were delivered in 1973 and the first SD40T–2s a few months later in 1974. The SD45T–2 was unique to SP,

but SD40T–2s were also ordered by the Denver & Rio Grande Western.

There were two variations of the SD40T–2, the standard model and those equipped for radio-controlled "slave" helper operations. Beginning in 1974 SP experimented with radio-controlled helpers as a way of eliminating manned helpers on some runs and distributing power through out a long, heavy train to ease drawbar stress. Through the implementation of radio-controlled locomotives, a single engineer could control locomotives at the head end and those in mid-train directly from his front-end cab position. Slave-equipped SD40T–2s featured a significantly longer front hood or nose that housed the radio-control equipment. Fourteen locomotives were set up for radio-slave service. Slave-helper operations were tried on several routes, including: the Sunset Route between Los Angeles and El Paso, Texas; Los Angeles to Bakersfield via the Tehachapis; and east of Klamath Falls, Oregon, on the Modoc Line. This first slave-master remote helper operation was a relatively short-lived concept on the SP. Difficulties with the radio communications system—including a disastrous wreck attributed to a serious communications failure in which helpers continued in full throttle after the head-end units had shutdown in an emergency brake application—resulted in all of the specially-equipped SD40T–2s being returned to the regular road pool. Twenty years later, SP would reintroduce remote

EMD's SD40-series was popular with a number of railroads, including SP which rostered several variations. Wearing an experimental paint scheme, No. 7432 at West Oakland on December 20, 1980, is a brand-new SD40E. That same year, the SP had been searching for a new corporate identity and experimented with a return to a livery that mimicked the famous *Daylight* colors. *Brian Jennison*

Though SP lost its enthusiasm for passenger transportation after the 1950s, in 1967 it took delivery of ten passenger-version SDP45s. The delivery of these units—one of which is shown leading the *Coast Daylight* at Paso Robles, California, in July 1969—are essentially what bumped the Alco PAs out of service. The 3,000-hp SDs generally worked the *Coast Daylight, San Joaquin Daylight,* the *Cascade,* and the *City of San Francisco* as far east as Ogden. *Mike Schafer*

helpers using an improved radio system that would prove much more successful.

In the late 1960s SP ordered ten SDP45s, the passenger variation of the SD45. Equipped with steam generators for train heating, these locomotives were initially used on SP's few remaining long-distance name trains except for the *Sunset Limited*, which tended to receive E- and F-units into the Amtrak era. Eventually the SDPs saw service on the San Francisco–San Jose commutes.

As well as its high-horsepower six-motor locomotives, SP operated a small fleet of intermediate horsepower six-motor EMDs. In addition to the previously mentioned SD35s there were six SD38–2s and 26 SD39s. The first batch of SD39s arrived in 1969. These locomotives used a 12-cylinder 645E3 prime mover and developed 2,300 hp. For many years they were used between Los Angeles/West Colton and Bakersfield over the Palmdale Cutoff and Tehachapis. They were also used on branch lines, such as the old Lone Pine branch that headed eastward from Mojave to a connection with the Trona Railroad at Searles, California.

In 1973 SP bought six SD38–2s for use in yard service. These highly specialized locomotives were designed for extremely high tractive effort at very low speeds, used a 16-cylinder 645-E3 prime mover, and were often paired with "slugs" (cabless, engineless, weighted locomotive counterparts with traction motors designed for pairing with a locomotive to provide greater tractive effort).

In the late 1970s SP expressed renewed interest in high-horsepower four-axle locomotives. Among other locomotives, it bought a few GP40Xs from EMD. After an order for additional SD40T–2s in the early 1980s, SP didn't purchase any new six-axle locomotives for more than a decade, instead focusing new purchases on its four-axle fleet and rebuilding its older EMD six-axles at its company shops. By the early 1990s, SP was one of the few American railroads that continued to buy new high-horsepower four axle locomotives—and did so until nearly the end SP's independent operations in the mid 1990s, ordering dozens of EMD GP40–2s, four-axle GEs, and EMD

In the late 1970s, SP acquired three GP40Xs from EMD, Nos. 7200–7202. These locomotives developed 3,500 hp using a 16-cylinder 645F prime mover, employed unusual looking model HT-B hi-adhesion trucks, and came equipped with air-dampers for improved airflow. The first in the series is shown at Blue Island, Illinois, in February 1978. *Steve Smedley*

Among the numerous types of four-axle, second-generation diesels acquired by SP were a fleet of 2,500-hp General Electric U25Bs, one of which poses side by side at West Oakland in 1976 with an Electro-Motive FP7 that SP had sold to Amtrak. The U25B represented GE's first and very successful entry into the road-locomotive business as an independent builder. *Brian Jennison*

Southern Pacific was one of only two American railroads to experiment with eight-axle second-generation diesel-electric locomotives. In 1964 it took delivery of three U50s from GE. These locomotives featured four sets of two-axle trucks in an unusual B-B-B-B wheel arrangement. Each locomotive was rated at 5,000 hp and represented essentially two U25Bs under a single hood. *Jim Boyd*

GP60s through the early 1990s. SP's GP60s were some of the last high-horsepower main-line four-axle freight locomotives ordered in the U.S. and were delivered at a time when the national trend for new freight locomotives had gone toward super high-horsepower (more than 4,000 hp per unit) six-axle locomotives. SP's later GP60s featured an improved dynamic braking system, marketed as "extended range" dynamic brakes. As with the GP35s and U25Bs, later four-axle locomotives were concentrated on the Sunset and Golden State routes and to a lesser extent the San Joaquin Valley and Shasta routes and primarily were used in intermodal service.

Not all second-generation motive power on the SP came from Electro-Motive, of course. Southern Pacific was an early buyer of General Electric diesels. In the 1940s it had bought a small fleet of GE switchers: 14 44-ton center-cabs and 21 70-ton end-cabs. The 70-ton switchers—classic shortline power—represented the largest such fleet owned by a Class I railroad and were primarily confined to the Oregon branches.

During the early years of diesel-electric development, GE was partners with Alco—a relationship that ended in 1953. Later in the 1950s, GE went on to develop its own road

freight locomotives using the Cooper-Bessemer FDL diesel engine design. In 1959, GE formally entered the new high-horsepower locomotive market with its U25B. ("U" for Universal line, "25" for 2,500 hp, and "B" indicating two-axle trucks). Between 1962 and 1964 SP purchased 65 U25Bs—for a short time the largest GE road fleet.

SP followed Union Pacific's lead and bought three of GE's eight-axle U50s. These unusual locomotives were noted for their enormous size, exceptionally high horsepower, and distinctive tall front cab. The U50 was essentially two U25Bs under a single hood, as it was powered by two 16-cylinder FDL engines and generated 5,000 hp. It sat on four two-axle trucks. The big locomotives were commonly operated in Sunset Route service in tandem with a pair of U25Bs.

Beginning in 1966 SP began purchasing General Electric six-axle locomotives, first ten U28Cs for Eagle Mountain (California) Ore Services, then a small fleet of 37 3,000-hp U30Cs, followed by 212 3,300-hp U33Cs—the single largest fleet of these locomotives. The big GEs were at home in the grassy hills and rocky canyons of southern California; Tehachapi, the Palmdale Cutoff, and the Coast Line were common domains for these locomotives where SP regularly operated them in sets of three on its long, heavy freights.

Early GE locomotives did not enjoy the same long life span that comparable EMD engines did. Where later EMDs were routinely rebuilt by the railroad and often served for 30 years or more, GE's only served for about dozen years, and some much less, before being sidelined, retired, and traded in or scrapped. By the late-1970s most of the U25Bs were off the active roster. Some were rebuilt into slugs. Four were re-manufactured in 1978 by Morrison-Knudsen; they were completely rebuilt, upgraded to 2,800 hp using Sulzer diesel engines, and designated TE70-4s. Painted in a splendid bright yellow and orange scheme dubbed "popsicles," the TE70-4s briefly operated in fast freight service, primarily between Los Angeles and Portland and handled one of the most demanding jobs on the system, the extra hot LABRT/BRLAT (Los Angeles–Brooklyn Yard [Portland] trailers) intermodal run. They were among the few U25Bs rebuilt for

service on any railroad and were not markedly successful. After just a few years these colorful locomotives were stored at Eugene. SP's six-motor GE's were also stored during the recession in the early 1980s and later retired without ever returning to road service.

Although SP continued to purchase GE products—including 15 2,300-hp B23–7s, along with 108 B30–7s and 19 B36–7s (plus one cabless B-unit) for Cotton Belt between 1978 and 1984—the railroad placed more significant orders from EMD until the mid 1990s. Through the 1980s, GE products were a curiosity on most of the railroad. They were rarely used on California lines north of L.A. and were an extreme rarity on the Overland Route. Many four-axle were assigned to the Cotton Belt and based at Pine Bluff, Arkansas.

In the late 1980s and early 1990s SP and its Cotton Belt subsidiary placed several orders for GE high-horsepower four-axle Dash 8 locomotives. These arrived on the property about the same time as EMD's similar GP60s and, like

SP's Vast Fleet of Electro-Motive Switchers

Often ignored and not nearly as impressive as their larger brethren, SP's EMD switchers have toiled away for generations in yards large and small, worked obscure branch lines, decaying remnants of SP's once vast inter-urban empires, winding industrial trackage, and even out on the mainline. Known as "goats" or "cruds", the EMD switchers remained an important part of SP's locomotive fleet into the 1990s, long after most railroads had largely

given up on this type of locomotive. Southern Pacific had a considerable fleet of early EMD switch engines including an SW1, NW2s, TR6s, SW7s, SW8s, SW9s, SW900s. and SW1200s. In 1967 the railroad began purchasing a large fleet of SW1500s. By 1973 SP had acquired more than 230 of the 1,500 hp switchers. Southern Pacific continued purchasing switchers through 1975 with its acquisition of 12 MP15s and 58 MP15ACs.

SP maintained a vast fleet of switchers and continued purchasing EMD switchers long after other railroads opted for more versatile locomotives. SP owned one of the largest rosters of EMD SW1500s, represented here by 2544. *Herb Johnson*

SP SD70M 9802 leads a westbound ASROM (Alton & Southern–Roseville Manifest) up the 1.02 percent grade at Alta Vista, Kansas, on October 9, 1994. SP purchased a small fleet of 25 EMD SD70Ms in 1994; these were the only EMD locomotive with safety cabs owned by SP. *Dan Munson*

Adding to SP's woes was the sad state of its locomotives, many of which were more than 25 years old and, despite rebuilding, suffered from old age and extremely heavy use. A typical SP freight might be hauled by as many as eight six-axle units, all in faded paint and covered in grime. Half of these engines might suffer road failure during the course of the run. Leased locomotives were so common, for a time at least one was seen on nearly every through freight. These leased locomotives weren't necessarily better than SP's own, being cast-away SD40s, SD45s, and GE six-motors that had already seen two decades or more of hard service for a previous owner. Every day dozens of trains were held at yards for lack of power, and at times the railroad was so desperate it would assign any available locomotive, regardless of original intended application, to help move trains over the road. Elderly SD9s, after years working Oregon branch lines, might be seen working as mid-train helpers to Cascade Summit; in the San Joaquin Valley an antique GP9, which for years had worked branchline local freights, would be called out of Bakersfield to help assist the "Oil Can" trains over Tehachapi Loop, its 1,750 hp adding its two cents' worth to a rake of straining six-motors.

In 1994 SP finally began to order large numbers of new and re-manufactured locomotives to help ease its motive-power crisis, and for the first time in more than ten years it bought new six-axle power. All were delivered in a variation of SP's 35-year-old scarlet-and-gray scheme, featuring "Southern Pacific" in large Rio Grande style "speed lettering" on their sides. This lettering modification had been introduced a few years earlier on GP40s re-manufactured by Morrison-Knudsen. Electro-Motive provided 25 SD70Ms while GE delivered 101 DASH9-44CWs. These were SP's first locomotives with the widenose 'safety cab' design, first ordered by Union Pacific in 1989, that had since become standard on most new American locomotives. Initially the SD70Ms were assigned to service between Portland and Los Angeles, while the GEs roamed the system. In the autumn of 1994, SP and regional railroad Wisconsin Central teamed up to handle unit taconite trains from Minnesota's iron range to Utah's Geneva Steel, winning this lucrative business away from arch competitor Union Pacific. To move these priority trains, SP assigned its newest, most reliable locomotives, and as a result its

earlier four-axle GEs, worked primarily east of L.A.. SP purchased 40 B39–8s in late 1987 and 55 DASH 8–40Bs (listed as B40–8s on some rosters) for Cotton Belt in 1988 and 1989.

SP IN TWILIGHT: MOTIVE-POWER DILEMMA

Following the stillborn merger with Santa Fe, SP's new locomotive purchases and its rebuilding program failed to keep pace with the railroad's need for motive power. The token purchases of four-axles for the Sunset Route hardly made a difference. By 1993 the railroad was suffering from enormous power shortages and was leasing more than 300 locomotives daily to help breach the shortage.

DASH 9s regularly ran north of Chicago to Fond du Lac, and sometimes Superior, Wisconsin in taconite service.

In 1994, SP also acquired 131 re-manufactured EMD six-motors from Morrison-Knudsen. While many of these locomotives were delivered in conventional SD45 hoods, they featured rebuilt 16-cylinder 645 prime movers and were rated at just 3,000 hp and were designated SD40M by the railroad.

In the mid-1990s, both General Electric and Electro-Motive developed practical alternating-current traction-motor technology and marketed new lines of diesel-electric locomotives, considered the most significant development in locomotive technology since the advent of the commercially produced diesel-electric. By employing a.c. traction motors, these new diesel-electric locomotives could generate significantly greater tractive effort, and operate at maximum power at much slower speeds than comparable d.c. traction locomotives. SP had been seeking to achieve this sort of improved pulling power with its ill-fated fleet of diesel-hydraulics in the early 1960s. Southern Pacific was among the first railroads to commit to large numbers of GE a.c. locomotives. Beginning in 1995, GE delivered 279 AC4400CWs to SP. Many of these locomotives were equipped for remote-slave operation using a vastly-improved control system. So 20 years after SP first experimented with remote locomotive operation, it reintroduced this labor-saving application. The AC4400CWs were at first largely assigned to mineral trains working coal and taconite runs in Colorado and Utah, but later roamed elsewhere around the railroad as needed. With the introduction of the AC4400CWs most of the DASH9s were reassigned to the Sunset Route and Cotton Belt Lines. The late-era purchase of the ACs concluded 125 years of Southern Pacific's distinctive locomotive policies. The first AC4400CWs were barely on the property when Union Pacific's pending acquisition of SP was announced, and some of these locomotives were less than a year old when melded into UP's growing motive-power fleet.

In its last years, SP operated a fleet of 380 GE six-axle locomotives with safety cabs. It ordered two distinctly different models: DASH9-44CW, a 4,400 hp model that used traditional direct-current traction motors; and AC4400CW, a modern locomotive using inverter technology and alternating-current traction motors. The DASH 9s are seen on the left, while AC4400CWs are on the right. The quickest way to identify each type on the SP was by the spacing between the letters on the nose. The DASH 9s display a noticeable gap, while ACs do not. *Steve Smedley*

Index